50 Tofu Recipes for Home

By: Kelly Johnson

Table of Contents

- Tofu Stir-Fry with Vegetables
- Crispy Tofu Nuggets
- Tofu Scramble Breakfast Tacos
- Baked Tofu with Teriyaki Glaze
- Tofu and Vegetable Kebabs
- Tofu Pad Thai
- Tofu Lettuce Wraps
- Tofu and Broccoli in Garlic Sauce
- Tofu and Spinach Stuffed Shells
- Tofu Coconut Curry
- Tofu Spring Rolls with Peanut Sauce
- Tofu and Mushroom Risotto
- Tofu Bolognese
- Tofu Caesar Salad
- Tofu Sushi Rolls
- BBQ Tofu Sandwiches
- Tofu Tikka Masala
- Tofu Satay Skewers
- Tofu Enchiladas
- Tofu Scallion Pancakes
- Tofu Frittata
- Tofu and Kale Salad with Sesame Dressing
- Tofu Banh Mi Sandwiches
- Tofu Mushroom Pot Pie
- Tofu BLT Wraps
- Tofu Ratatouille
- Tofu and Corn Chowder
- Tofu Katsu
- Tofu Stroganoff
- Tofu Tikki Burger
- Tofu Thai Green Curry
- Tofu and Black Bean Tacos
- Tofu and Chickpea Tagine
- Tofu Scampi
- Tofu and Avocado Quesadillas

- Tofu Chive Dumplings
- Tofu and Sweet Potato Hash
- Tofu Miso Soup
- Tofu Pesto Pasta
- Tofu Stuffed Peppers
- Tofu Caesar Wraps
- Tofu Kimchi Fried Rice
- Tofu and Eggplant Parmesan
- Tofu Meatballs
- Tofu Cacciatore
- Tofu Sloppy Joes
- Tofu Spinach Lasagna
- Tofu Pita Pockets
- Tofu Waldorf Salad
- Tofu Lemon Bars

Tofu Stir-Fry with Vegetables

Ingredients:

- 14 oz (400g) firm tofu, drained and pressed
- 2 tablespoons soy sauce (or tamari for gluten-free)
- 1 tablespoon rice vinegar
- 1 tablespoon hoisin sauce
- 1 tablespoon sesame oil
- 2 tablespoons vegetable oil
- 3 cloves garlic, minced
- 1-inch piece of ginger, minced
- 1 red bell pepper, sliced
- 1 yellow bell pepper, sliced
- 1 small broccoli crown, cut into florets
- 1 medium carrot, thinly sliced
- 1 cup snow peas, trimmed
- Salt and pepper, to taste
- Cooked rice or noodles, for serving
- Optional garnishes: chopped green onions, sesame seeds

Instructions:

1. Prepare the Tofu:
    - Drain the tofu and press it to remove excess moisture. You can do this by wrapping the tofu block in paper towels or a clean kitchen towel and placing a heavy object on top for about 20-30 minutes. Then, cut the tofu into cubes.
2. Make the Stir-Fry Sauce:
    - In a small bowl, whisk together the soy sauce, rice vinegar, hoisin sauce, and sesame oil. Set aside.
3. Stir-Fry the Tofu:
    - Heat 1 tablespoon of vegetable oil in a large skillet or wok over medium-high heat. Add the tofu cubes in a single layer. Cook for 4-5 minutes, flipping occasionally, until the tofu is golden and slightly crispy. Remove the tofu from the skillet and set aside.
4. Cook the Vegetables:
    - In the same skillet, add another tablespoon of vegetable oil if needed. Add the minced garlic and ginger, and sauté for about 30 seconds until fragrant.

- Add the sliced bell peppers, broccoli florets, carrot slices, and snow peas to the skillet. Stir-fry for 4-5 minutes until the vegetables are tender-crisp.
5. Combine Everything:
    - Return the cooked tofu to the skillet. Pour the stir-fry sauce over the tofu and vegetables. Toss everything together gently to coat evenly. Cook for another 1-2 minutes to heat through.
6. Serve:
    - Serve the tofu stir-fry over cooked rice or noodles. Garnish with chopped green onions and sesame seeds if desired.

Enjoy your delicious tofu stir-fry with vegetables! This dish is versatile, so feel free to customize it with your favorite vegetables or additional seasonings. It's a perfect healthy and satisfying meal.

Crispy Tofu Nuggets

Ingredients:

- 14 oz (400g) firm tofu
- 1/4 cup all-purpose flour (or cornstarch for gluten-free)
- 1/2 teaspoon garlic powder
- 1/2 teaspoon onion powder
- 1/2 teaspoon paprika
- 1/2 teaspoon salt
- 1/4 teaspoon black pepper
- 1 cup breadcrumbs (regular or panko)
- 2 eggs, beaten (or use a plant-based milk like almond milk for vegan option)
- Cooking oil (such as vegetable oil or canola oil), for frying
- Dipping sauce of choice (such as sweet chili sauce, barbecue sauce, or ranch dressing)

Instructions:

1. Prepare the Tofu:
    - Drain the tofu and press it to remove excess moisture. You can do this by wrapping the tofu block in paper towels or a clean kitchen towel and placing a heavy object on top for about 20-30 minutes. Once pressed, cut the tofu into small nugget-sized pieces.
2. Set Up Dredging Station:
    - In one shallow bowl, mix together the all-purpose flour (or cornstarch), garlic powder, onion powder, paprika, salt, and black pepper.
    - In another shallow bowl, place the beaten eggs (or plant-based milk).
    - In a third shallow bowl, spread out the breadcrumbs.
3. Coat the Tofu Nuggets:
    - Take each piece of tofu and dredge it first in the seasoned flour mixture, shaking off any excess.
    - Dip the floured tofu piece into the beaten eggs (or plant-based milk), allowing any excess to drip off.
    - Coat the tofu nugget evenly with breadcrumbs, pressing gently to adhere.
4. Fry the Tofu Nuggets:
    - Heat about 1/2 inch of cooking oil in a large skillet over medium-high heat.
    - Once the oil is hot (around 350°F or 180°C), carefully place the coated tofu nuggets into the skillet in a single layer, without overcrowding.

- Fry the nuggets for 2-3 minutes on each side, or until golden brown and crispy. Use tongs to turn them gently.
5. Drain and Serve:
    - Once crispy and golden, transfer the tofu nuggets to a plate lined with paper towels to drain excess oil.
    - Serve the crispy tofu nuggets hot with your favorite dipping sauce on the side.

Enjoy these crispy tofu nuggets as a delicious snack or part of a meal. They are crunchy on the outside and soft on the inside, making them a delightful vegetarian treat!

Tofu Scramble Breakfast Tacos

Ingredients:

- 14 oz (400g) firm tofu, drained and pressed
- 1 tablespoon olive oil or cooking oil of choice
- 1 small onion, finely chopped
- 2 garlic cloves, minced
- 1 bell pepper (any color), diced
- 1 teaspoon ground cumin
- 1/2 teaspoon turmeric (for color)
- Salt and pepper, to taste
- Optional toppings: chopped fresh cilantro, sliced avocado, salsa, hot sauce, diced tomatoes, shredded cheese (vegan or dairy), sour cream (vegan or dairy), lime wedges
- 6-8 small corn or flour tortillas, warmed

Instructions:

1. Prepare the Tofu:
    - Drain the tofu and press it to remove excess moisture. Crumble the pressed tofu into small pieces resembling scrambled eggs.
2. Sauté the Vegetables:
    - Heat the olive oil in a large skillet over medium heat. Add the chopped onion and sauté for 2-3 minutes until translucent.
    - Add the minced garlic and diced bell pepper to the skillet. Cook for another 3-4 minutes until the vegetables are tender.
3. Make the Tofu Scramble:
    - Push the sautéed vegetables to one side of the skillet. Add the crumbled tofu to the skillet, spreading it out in an even layer.
    - Sprinkle the ground cumin and turmeric over the tofu. Gently mix everything together to incorporate the spices and evenly distribute the tofu with the vegetables.
    - Cook for 5-7 minutes, stirring occasionally, until the tofu is heated through and slightly golden. Season with salt and pepper to taste.
4. Assemble the Tacos:
    - Warm the tortillas in a dry skillet or microwave until soft and pliable.
    - Spoon the tofu scramble mixture onto each tortilla.

- Top the tacos with your favorite toppings such as chopped fresh cilantro, sliced avocado, salsa, hot sauce, diced tomatoes, shredded cheese, or sour cream.
5. Serve and Enjoy:
    - Serve the tofu scramble breakfast tacos immediately.
    - Squeeze fresh lime juice over the tacos for an extra burst of flavor if desired.

These tofu scramble breakfast tacos are versatile, flavorful, and packed with protein. Customize them with your preferred toppings and enjoy a delicious vegetarian breakfast or brunch!

Baked Tofu with Teriyaki Glaze

Ingredients:

- 14 oz (400g) firm tofu, drained and pressed
- 1/3 cup soy sauce (or tamari for gluten-free)
- 1/4 cup water
- 3 tablespoons brown sugar
- 2 tablespoons rice vinegar
- 2 cloves garlic, minced
- 1 teaspoon grated fresh ginger
- 1 tablespoon cornstarch (or arrowroot powder)
- Sesame seeds, for garnish (optional)
- Chopped green onions, for garnish (optional)

Instructions:

1. Prepare the Tofu:
    - Preheat your oven to 400°F (200°C).
    - Drain the tofu and press it to remove excess moisture. You can do this by wrapping the tofu block in paper towels or a clean kitchen towel and placing a heavy object on top for about 20-30 minutes. Once pressed, cut the tofu into cubes or slices.
2. Make the Teriyaki Glaze:
    - In a small saucepan, combine the soy sauce, water, brown sugar, rice vinegar, minced garlic, and grated ginger. Stir well and bring to a simmer over medium heat.
    - In a separate small bowl, mix the cornstarch with 1 tablespoon of water to create a slurry. Add the cornstarch slurry to the simmering sauce, stirring constantly until the sauce thickens slightly. Remove from heat.
3. Coat the Tofu with Glaze:
    - Place the tofu cubes or slices in a single layer on a baking sheet lined with parchment paper or lightly greased.
    - Brush or spoon the teriyaki glaze over the tofu, coating each piece evenly.
4. Bake the Tofu:
    - Place the baking sheet in the preheated oven and bake for 20-25 minutes, or until the tofu is golden and slightly caramelized around the edges, flipping the tofu halfway through baking for even cooking.
5. Serve:
    - Once baked, remove the tofu from the oven.

- Transfer the baked tofu to a serving dish and garnish with sesame seeds and chopped green onions if desired.
- Serve the baked tofu with teriyaki glaze as a delicious main dish or protein-packed addition to salads, stir-fries, rice bowls, or noodles.

Enjoy this baked tofu with homemade teriyaki glaze for a flavorful and satisfying meal. It's perfect for both lunch and dinner, and you can easily customize it with your favorite sides and accompaniments.

Tofu and Vegetable Kebabs

Ingredients:

- 14 oz (400g) firm tofu, drained and pressed
- 1 red bell pepper, cut into chunks
- 1 green bell pepper, cut into chunks
- 1 zucchini, sliced into rounds
- 1 red onion, cut into chunks
- Cherry tomatoes
- For the marinade:
    - 1/4 cup soy sauce (or tamari for gluten-free)
    - 2 tablespoons olive oil
    - 2 tablespoons maple syrup or honey
    - 2 cloves garlic, minced
    - 1 teaspoon grated fresh ginger
    - 1 tablespoon rice vinegar
    - Salt and pepper, to taste
    - Wooden or metal skewers (if using wooden skewers, soak them in water for at least 30 minutes before using)

Instructions:

1. Prepare the Tofu:
    - Drain the tofu and press it to remove excess moisture. Cut the tofu into cubes or rectangles that are roughly the same size as the vegetable chunks.
2. Make the Marinade:
    - In a bowl, whisk together soy sauce, olive oil, maple syrup (or honey), minced garlic, grated ginger, rice vinegar, salt, and pepper.
3. Marinate the Tofu and Vegetables:
    - Place the tofu cubes and prepared vegetables (bell peppers, zucchini, red onion, cherry tomatoes) in a large bowl.
    - Pour the marinade over the tofu and vegetables. Gently toss to coat everything evenly. Let it marinate for at least 30 minutes, or cover and refrigerate for up to 4 hours, tossing occasionally.
4. Assemble the Kebabs:
    - Preheat your grill or oven to medium-high heat (if using the oven, preheat to 400°F or 200°C).

- Thread the marinated tofu cubes and vegetables onto skewers, alternating the tofu with the vegetables.
5. Cook the Kebabs:
    - Grill the kebabs on the preheated grill, turning occasionally, for about 10-15 minutes or until the tofu and vegetables are nicely charred and cooked through.
    - If baking in the oven, place the kebabs on a baking sheet lined with parchment paper or lightly greased. Bake for 20-25 minutes, turning halfway through cooking.
6. Serve:
    - Once cooked, remove the tofu and vegetable kebabs from the grill or oven.
    - Serve the kebabs hot with rice, quinoa, or couscous, and enjoy with your favorite dipping sauce or a squeeze of fresh lemon or lime juice.

These tofu and vegetable kebabs are flavorful, colorful, and packed with nutrients. They make a fantastic main dish for vegetarian meals or as a tasty addition to any barbecue or gathering. Customize the vegetables based on your preferences and enjoy this delicious dish!

Tofu Lettuce Wraps

Ingredients:

- 14 oz (400g) firm tofu, drained and pressed
- 2 tablespoons soy sauce (or tamari for gluten-free)
- 1 tablespoon hoisin sauce
- 1 tablespoon rice vinegar
- 1 tablespoon sesame oil
- 2 tablespoons vegetable oil, divided
- 2 cloves garlic, minced
- 1-inch piece of ginger, grated
- 1 small onion, finely chopped
- 1 bell pepper (any color), finely chopped
- 1 carrot, grated or finely chopped
- 1/2 cup water chestnuts, drained and finely chopped
- 2-3 green onions, chopped
- Salt and pepper, to taste
- 1 head of iceberg or butter lettuce, leaves separated
- Optional garnishes: chopped peanuts, cilantro leaves, sriracha sauce

Instructions:

1. Prepare the Tofu:
    - Drain the tofu and press it to remove excess moisture. Crumble the pressed tofu into small pieces resembling ground meat.
2. Make the Sauce:
    - In a small bowl, whisk together soy sauce, hoisin sauce, rice vinegar, and sesame oil. Set aside.
3. Stir-Fry the Tofu and Vegetables:
    - Heat 1 tablespoon of vegetable oil in a large skillet or wok over medium-high heat.
    - Add minced garlic and grated ginger to the skillet. Sauté for about 30 seconds until fragrant.
    - Add chopped onion and bell pepper to the skillet. Cook for 2-3 minutes until vegetables start to soften.
    - Add the crumbled tofu to the skillet. Stir-fry for 4-5 minutes, breaking up any large chunks, until the tofu is lightly browned.
4. Combine Everything:

- Pour the sauce over the tofu and vegetables in the skillet. Stir well to coat everything evenly.
- Add grated carrot, water chestnuts, and chopped green onions to the skillet. Stir-fry for another 2-3 minutes until heated through.
- Season with salt and pepper to taste.

5. Assemble the Lettuce Wraps:
    - Spoon the tofu and vegetable mixture into individual lettuce leaves, creating wraps.
    - Top the wraps with chopped peanuts, cilantro leaves, and a drizzle of sriracha sauce if desired.
6. Serve and Enjoy:
    - Arrange the tofu lettuce wraps on a platter and serve immediately.
    - Enjoy these delicious and healthy tofu lettuce wraps as a light meal or appetizer.

Feel free to customize the filling with your favorite vegetables and adjust the seasoning according to your taste preferences. These tofu lettuce wraps are versatile, flavorful, and perfect for a quick and nutritious meal!

Tofu and Broccoli in Garlic Sauce

Ingredients:

- 14 oz (400g) firm tofu, drained and pressed
- 1 head of broccoli, cut into florets
- 4 cloves garlic, minced
- 1-inch piece of ginger, grated
- 2 tablespoons soy sauce (or tamari for gluten-free)
- 1 tablespoon hoisin sauce
- 1 tablespoon rice vinegar
- 1 tablespoon sesame oil
- 2 tablespoons vegetable oil
- 1 tablespoon cornstarch (or arrowroot powder) dissolved in 2 tablespoons water
- Red pepper flakes (optional), for heat
- Salt and pepper, to taste
- Cooked rice or noodles, for serving
- Optional garnish: sliced green onions, sesame seeds

Instructions:

1. Prepare the Tofu:
    - Drain the tofu and press it to remove excess moisture. Cut the tofu into cubes.
2. Blanch the Broccoli:
    - Bring a pot of water to a boil. Add the broccoli florets and cook for 2-3 minutes, until they are bright green and slightly tender. Drain and set aside.
3. Make the Sauce:
    - In a small bowl, whisk together soy sauce, hoisin sauce, rice vinegar, sesame oil, and dissolved cornstarch. Set aside.
4. Stir-Fry the Tofu and Vegetables:
    - Heat vegetable oil in a large skillet or wok over medium-high heat.
    - Add the tofu cubes to the skillet and cook for 4-5 minutes, flipping occasionally, until they are golden and crispy on all sides. Remove tofu from the skillet and set aside.
5. Cook the Garlic and Ginger:
    - In the same skillet, add minced garlic and grated ginger. Sauté for about 30 seconds until fragrant.
6. Combine and Simmer:
    - Return the cooked tofu to the skillet with the garlic and ginger.

- Add the blanched broccoli florets to the skillet.
- Pour the prepared sauce over the tofu and broccoli in the skillet. Stir well to coat everything evenly.
- Allow the sauce to simmer for 2-3 minutes, stirring occasionally, until it thickens and coats the tofu and broccoli.
- If desired, add a pinch of red pepper flakes for a bit of heat.
- Season with salt and pepper to taste.

7. Serve:
    - Serve the tofu and broccoli in garlic sauce hot over cooked rice or noodles.
    - Garnish with sliced green onions and sesame seeds if desired.

Enjoy this delicious tofu and broccoli in garlic sauce as a flavorful and satisfying vegetarian meal! Feel free to adjust the seasoning and spice level according to your taste preferences.

Tofu and Spinach Stuffed Shells

Ingredients:

- 20-24 jumbo pasta shells
- 14 oz (400g) firm tofu, drained and pressed
- 1 cup frozen chopped spinach, thawed and drained
- 1/2 cup grated Parmesan cheese (use vegan Parmesan if preferred)
- 1/4 cup chopped fresh basil (or 1 tablespoon dried basil)
- 2 cloves garlic, minced
- 1 tablespoon olive oil
- Salt and pepper, to taste
- 2 cups marinara sauce
- Shredded mozzarella cheese (optional, use vegan cheese if preferred)
- Fresh parsley, chopped, for garnish (optional)

Instructions:

1. Cook the Pasta Shells:
    - Bring a large pot of salted water to a boil. Cook the jumbo pasta shells according to the package instructions until al dente. Drain and set aside.
2. Prepare the Tofu Filling:
    - In a large mixing bowl, crumble the drained and pressed tofu using your hands or a fork.
    - Add the thawed and drained chopped spinach, grated Parmesan cheese (or vegan alternative), chopped fresh basil, minced garlic, olive oil, salt, and pepper to the crumbled tofu. Mix well until all ingredients are combined.
3. Stuff the Pasta Shells:
    - Preheat the oven to 375°F (190°C).
    - Spread a thin layer of marinara sauce on the bottom of a 9x13-inch baking dish.
    - Using a spoon, fill each cooked pasta shell generously with the tofu and spinach mixture. Arrange the stuffed shells in the baking dish.
4. Assemble and Bake:
    - Once all the shells are stuffed and placed in the baking dish, spoon the remaining marinara sauce over the top of the shells, covering them evenly.
    - If desired, sprinkle shredded mozzarella cheese (or vegan cheese) on top of the shells.
5. Bake the Stuffed Shells:

- Cover the baking dish with aluminum foil and bake in the preheated oven for 20-25 minutes, or until the shells are heated through and the sauce is bubbly.
- Remove the foil during the last 5 minutes of baking to allow the cheese to melt and slightly brown.

6. Serve:
    - Once baked, remove the stuffed shells from the oven.
    - Garnish with chopped fresh parsley for added color and flavor.
    - Serve hot and enjoy these delicious tofu and spinach stuffed shells as a main course.

These tofu and spinach stuffed shells are flavorful, satisfying, and perfect for vegetarians or anyone looking for a tasty meatless meal. Serve them with a side salad or garlic bread for a complete dinner. Enjoy!

Tofu Coconut Curry

Ingredients:

- 14 oz (400g) firm tofu, drained and pressed
- 1 tablespoon vegetable oil
- 1 onion, finely chopped
- 3 cloves garlic, minced
- 1 tablespoon grated ginger
- 1 red bell pepper, sliced
- 1 yellow bell pepper, sliced
- 2 tablespoons red curry paste
- 1 can (14 oz or 400ml) coconut milk
- 1 tablespoon soy sauce (or tamari for gluten-free)
- 1 tablespoon brown sugar (optional, adjust to taste)
- Juice of 1 lime
- Salt and pepper, to taste
- Fresh cilantro, chopped, for garnish
- Cooked rice or naan bread, for serving

Instructions:

1. Prepare the Tofu:
    - Drain the tofu and press it to remove excess moisture. Cut the tofu into cubes.
2. Sauté the Aromatics:
    - Heat the vegetable oil in a large skillet or pot over medium heat. Add the chopped onion and sauté for 2-3 minutes until softened.
    - Add the minced garlic and grated ginger to the skillet. Sauté for another 1-2 minutes until fragrant.
3. Add the Vegetables and Curry Paste:
    - Add the sliced bell peppers to the skillet. Cook for 3-4 minutes until the peppers start to soften.
    - Stir in the red curry paste and cook for 1 minute, stirring constantly to coat the vegetables in the curry paste.
4. Make the Coconut Curry:
    - Pour in the coconut milk and stir well to combine with the curry paste and vegetables.
    - Add soy sauce and brown sugar (if using) to the skillet. Stir to mix.

- Bring the curry to a simmer and let it cook for 5 minutes, allowing the flavors to meld together.
5. Add the Tofu and Seasonings:
    - Gently add the tofu cubes to the simmering curry. Stir carefully to coat the tofu with the sauce.
    - Squeeze in the juice of one lime. Season with salt and pepper to taste.
6. Serve:
    - Serve the tofu coconut curry hot over cooked rice or with naan bread.
    - Garnish with chopped fresh cilantro.
    - Enjoy your flavorful and creamy tofu coconut curry!

Feel free to adjust the spiciness level by adding more or less red curry paste. You can also customize the vegetables based on your preferences. This tofu coconut curry is a satisfying and comforting dish that's perfect for a weeknight dinner. Enjoy!

Tofu Spring Rolls with Peanut Sauce

Ingredients:

For Tofu Spring Rolls:

- 8-10 rice paper spring roll wrappers
- 14 oz (400g) firm tofu, drained and sliced into thin strips
- 1 cup shredded lettuce
- 1 cup shredded carrots
- 1 cucumber, julienned
- 1 bell pepper (any color), julienned
- 1/4 cup fresh mint leaves
- 1/4 cup fresh cilantro leaves
- Rice vermicelli noodles, cooked according to package instructions (optional)
- Warm water, for soaking rice paper wrappers

For Peanut Sauce:

- 1/3 cup creamy peanut butter
- 2 tablespoons soy sauce (or tamari for gluten-free)
- 1 tablespoon rice vinegar
- 1 tablespoon maple syrup or honey
- 1 clove garlic, minced
- 1 teaspoon grated ginger
- Warm water, as needed to thin the sauce

Instructions:

1. Prepare Tofu and Vegetables:
    - Drain the tofu and slice it into thin strips.
    - Shred the lettuce and carrots. Julienne the cucumber and bell pepper.
    - Prepare fresh mint leaves and cilantro leaves.
2. Cook Rice Vermicelli (if using):
    - Cook rice vermicelli noodles according to package instructions. Drain and set aside.
3. Prepare Peanut Sauce:
    - In a small bowl, whisk together peanut butter, soy sauce, rice vinegar, maple syrup (or honey), minced garlic, and grated ginger.

- Add warm water gradually to the peanut butter mixture, stirring continuously, until you reach a smooth and creamy consistency. Set aside.
4. Assemble Tofu Spring Rolls:
    - Fill a shallow dish or large bowl with warm water.
    - Dip one rice paper wrapper into the warm water for a few seconds until it softens.
    - Place the softened rice paper wrapper on a clean surface.
    - Arrange a few strips of tofu, shredded lettuce, shredded carrots, cucumber, bell pepper, mint leaves, cilantro leaves, and cooked rice vermicelli (if using) in the center of the rice paper wrapper.
5. Roll the Spring Rolls:
    - Fold the bottom of the rice paper wrapper over the filling.
    - Fold in the sides, then continue rolling tightly to form a spring roll.
    - Repeat with the remaining rice paper wrappers and filling ingredients.
6. Serve with Peanut Sauce:
    - Arrange the tofu spring rolls on a serving platter.
    - Serve the peanut sauce in a small bowl alongside the spring rolls for dipping.
7. Enjoy:
    - Enjoy these tofu spring rolls with peanut sauce as a delicious appetizer or light meal.
    - Dip the spring rolls into the peanut sauce and savor the fresh and crunchy flavors!

Feel free to customize the filling of the spring rolls with your favorite vegetables or herbs. You can also add cooked shrimp, chicken, or additional tofu for protein. These tofu spring rolls are best enjoyed fresh and are perfect for a healthy and satisfying snack or lunch. Enjoy!

Tofu and Mushroom Risotto

Ingredients:

- 14 oz (400g) firm tofu, drained and cut into small cubes
- 2 cups Arborio rice
- 1 onion, finely chopped
- 2 cloves garlic, minced
- 8 oz (225g) mushrooms (such as cremini or button), sliced
- 4 cups vegetable broth
- 1 cup dry white wine (optional; can substitute with additional vegetable broth)
- 1/2 cup grated Parmesan cheese (use vegan Parmesan if preferred)
- 2 tablespoons unsalted butter or olive oil
- 2 tablespoons chopped fresh parsley
- Salt and pepper, to taste

Instructions:

1. Prepare the Tofu:
    - Drain the tofu and cut it into small cubes. You can optionally press the tofu to remove excess moisture.
2. Sauté the Tofu:
    - In a large skillet or pan, heat 1 tablespoon of butter or olive oil over medium-high heat.
    - Add the tofu cubes and cook until golden and crispy on all sides. Remove from the pan and set aside.
3. Cook the Mushrooms:
    - In the same skillet, add another tablespoon of butter or olive oil if needed.
    - Add the chopped onion and minced garlic. Sauté for 2-3 minutes until softened and fragrant.
    - Add the sliced mushrooms to the skillet and cook for 5-6 minutes until they release their moisture and start to brown. Season with salt and pepper.
4. Toast the Rice:
    - Add the Arborio rice to the skillet with the mushrooms, onion, and garlic. Stir to coat the rice in the oil and toast for 1-2 minutes.
5. Cook the Risotto:
    - Pour in the dry white wine (if using) and stir until the liquid is absorbed by the rice.

- Begin adding the vegetable broth, one ladleful at a time, stirring frequently and allowing the rice to absorb the liquid before adding more. Continue this process for about 18-20 minutes or until the rice is creamy and cooked al dente.
6. Finish the Risotto:
    - Stir in the cooked tofu cubes and grated Parmesan cheese.
    - Taste and adjust seasoning with salt and pepper as needed.
7. Serve:
    - Garnish the tofu and mushroom risotto with chopped fresh parsley.
    - Serve hot and enjoy this creamy and flavorful dish!

This tofu and mushroom risotto is rich, creamy, and packed with savory flavors. It's perfect for a special dinner or anytime you're craving a comforting meal. Serve it with a side salad or steamed vegetables for a complete and satisfying dish. Enjoy!

Tofu Bolognese

Ingredients:

- 14 oz (400g) firm tofu, drained and crumbled
- 2 tablespoons olive oil
- 1 onion, finely chopped
- 2 carrots, finely chopped
- 2 celery stalks, finely chopped
- 3 cloves garlic, minced
- 1 teaspoon dried oregano
- 1 teaspoon dried basil
- 1/2 teaspoon dried thyme
- 1/2 teaspoon red pepper flakes (adjust to taste)
- Salt and black pepper, to taste
- 1 can (14 oz or 400g) crushed tomatoes
- 1/2 cup tomato paste
- 1 cup vegetable broth or water
- 1 tablespoon soy sauce or tamari (for umami flavor)
- 2 tablespoons chopped fresh parsley, for garnish
- Cooked pasta, such as spaghetti or fettuccine, for serving
- Grated Parmesan cheese or vegan Parmesan, for topping (optional)

Instructions:

1. Prepare the Tofu:
    - Drain the tofu and crumble it into small pieces using your hands or a fork.
2. Sauté the Vegetables:
    - Heat the olive oil in a large skillet or pot over medium heat.
    - Add the chopped onion, carrots, and celery. Cook for 5-6 minutes until the vegetables start to soften.
3. Add Garlic and Spices:
    - Add the minced garlic, dried oregano, dried basil, dried thyme, red pepper flakes, salt, and black pepper to the skillet. Stir and cook for another minute until fragrant.
4. Cook the Tofu:
    - Push the sautéed vegetables to one side of the skillet and add the crumbled tofu to the empty side.
    - Cook the tofu for 5-6 minutes, stirring occasionally, until it starts to brown slightly.

5. Simmer the Sauce:
   - Stir in the crushed tomatoes, tomato paste, vegetable broth (or water), and soy sauce (or tamari) into the skillet with the tofu and vegetables.
   - Bring the sauce to a simmer, then reduce the heat to low. Let it simmer gently for 20-25 minutes, stirring occasionally, until the sauce thickens and the flavors meld together.
6. Adjust Seasoning and Serve:
   - Taste and adjust seasoning with more salt, pepper, or herbs if needed.
   - Serve the Tofu Bolognese sauce over cooked pasta (such as spaghetti or fettuccine).
   - Garnish with chopped fresh parsley and grated Parmesan cheese or vegan Parmesan, if desired.
7. Enjoy:
   - Serve hot and enjoy this delicious and satisfying Tofu Bolognese!

This Tofu Bolognese is a hearty and flavorful vegetarian alternative to traditional meat-based Bolognese sauce. It's perfect for a cozy dinner and can be enjoyed with your favorite pasta. Feel free to customize the recipe by adding extra vegetables or adjusting the seasonings to suit your taste. Enjoy!

Tofu Caesar Salad

Ingredients:

For the Tofu:

- 14 oz (400g) firm tofu, drained and pressed
- 2 tablespoons olive oil
- 1 tablespoon soy sauce or tamari
- 1 teaspoon garlic powder
- Salt and pepper, to taste

For the Caesar Dressing:

- 1/2 cup mayonnaise (regular or vegan)
- 2 tablespoons grated Parmesan cheese (or vegan Parmesan)
- 1 tablespoon Dijon mustard
- 2 cloves garlic, minced
- 2 tablespoons fresh lemon juice
- 1 teaspoon Worcestershire sauce (omit for vegetarian or use vegan Worcestershire)
- Salt and pepper, to taste
- Water, as needed to thin the dressing

For the Salad:

- Romaine lettuce, washed and chopped
- Croutons (store-bought or homemade)
- Additional grated Parmesan cheese (or vegan Parmesan), for topping

Instructions:

1. Prepare the Tofu:
    - Preheat the oven to 400°F (200°C).
    - Cut the pressed tofu into cubes or strips.
    - In a bowl, whisk together olive oil, soy sauce (or tamari), garlic powder, salt, and pepper.
    - Toss the tofu cubes in the marinade until evenly coated.
    - Spread the tofu cubes on a baking sheet lined with parchment paper.

- Bake for 25-30 minutes, flipping halfway through, until the tofu is golden and crispy. Set aside to cool slightly.
2. Make the Caesar Dressing:
    - In a bowl, combine mayonnaise, grated Parmesan cheese, Dijon mustard, minced garlic, fresh lemon juice, Worcestershire sauce (if using), salt, and pepper.
    - Whisk until smooth and creamy. If the dressing is too thick, add water a tablespoon at a time until desired consistency is reached. Taste and adjust seasoning as needed.
3. Assemble the Salad:
    - In a large bowl, toss chopped Romaine lettuce with desired amount of Caesar dressing until evenly coated.
    - Add crispy tofu cubes and croutons to the salad.
    - Toss gently to combine.
4. Serve:
    - Divide the tofu Caesar salad onto serving plates.
    - Top each serving with additional grated Parmesan cheese (or vegan Parmesan) if desired.
    - Serve immediately and enjoy!

This tofu Caesar salad is packed with flavor and textures, from the crispy baked tofu to the creamy Caesar dressing. It's perfect for a light lunch or dinner, and you can customize it with your favorite salad additions. Feel free to add cherry tomatoes, avocado slices, or roasted chickpeas for extra protein. Enjoy this delicious and satisfying tofu Caesar salad!

Tofu Sushi Rolls

Ingredients:

For Sushi Rice:

- 1 cup sushi rice (short-grain Japanese rice)
- 1 1/4 cups water
- 2 tablespoons rice vinegar
- 1 tablespoon sugar
- 1/2 teaspoon salt

For Tofu Filling:

- 14 oz (400g) firm tofu, drained and pressed
- 2 tablespoons soy sauce or tamari
- 1 tablespoon sesame oil
- 1 tablespoon rice vinegar
- 1 tablespoon maple syrup or agave syrup
- 1 clove garlic, minced
- 1/2 teaspoon grated ginger
- Sesame seeds, for garnish

For Sushi Rolls:

- Nori (seaweed) sheets
- Thinly sliced vegetables (cucumber, avocado, carrot, bell pepper)
- Pickled ginger, wasabi, soy sauce, for serving (optional)

Instructions:

1. Prepare Sushi Rice:
    - Rinse the sushi rice in cold water until the water runs clear. Drain well.
    - In a rice cooker or pot, combine the rice and water. Cook according to the rice cooker instructions or bring to a boil, then reduce heat to low, cover, and simmer for 15-20 minutes until the rice is cooked and water is absorbed.
    - In a small bowl, mix rice vinegar, sugar, and salt until dissolved. Stir the vinegar mixture into the cooked rice while it's still hot. Let the rice cool to room temperature.

2. **Prepare Tofu Filling:**
    - Cut the pressed tofu into thin strips or cubes.
    - In a bowl, whisk together soy sauce (or tamari), sesame oil, rice vinegar, maple syrup (or agave syrup), minced garlic, and grated ginger.
    - Add the tofu to the marinade and toss to coat. Let it marinate for at least 15-20 minutes.
3. **Cook Tofu:**
    - Heat a non-stick skillet over medium heat. Add the marinated tofu (reserve marinade) and cook for 5-7 minutes until tofu is golden brown and caramelized, stirring occasionally. Remove from heat.
4. **Assemble Sushi Rolls:**
    - Place a nori sheet on a bamboo sushi mat or a clean kitchen towel.
    - Spread a thin layer of sushi rice evenly over the nori sheet, leaving a small border along the edges.
    - Arrange a layer of tofu strips and sliced vegetables (cucumber, avocado, carrot, bell pepper) across the bottom third of the rice-covered nori sheet.
5. **Roll Sushi:**
    - Roll the nori sheet tightly from the bottom using the bamboo sushi mat or kitchen towel to help shape the roll.
    - Seal the edge with a little water to ensure it sticks together.
6. **Slice and Serve:**
    - Using a sharp knife, slice the sushi roll into 6-8 pieces.
    - Sprinkle sesame seeds on top of the sushi rolls for garnish.
7. **Serve:**
    - Serve tofu sushi rolls with pickled ginger, wasabi, and soy sauce on the side for dipping, if desired.

Enjoy these delicious and healthy tofu sushi rolls as a nutritious snack or light meal. You can customize the fillings based on your preference and serve them with your favorite sushi condiments. Have fun making and eating homemade vegan sushi!

BBQ Tofu Sandwiches

Ingredients:

For BBQ Tofu:

- 14 oz (400g) firm tofu, drained and pressed
- 1 cup BBQ sauce (use your favorite store-bought or homemade)
- 2 tablespoons olive oil
- Salt and pepper, to taste

For Sandwiches:

- Hamburger buns or sandwich rolls
- Coleslaw (store-bought or homemade)
- Sliced pickles
- Red onion, thinly sliced (optional)
- Lettuce leaves

Instructions:

1. Prepare BBQ Tofu:
   - Preheat the oven to 400°F (200°C).
   - Cut the pressed tofu into thick slices or cubes.
   - In a bowl, toss the tofu with olive oil, salt, and pepper.
   - Place the tofu on a baking sheet lined with parchment paper.
   - Bake for 20 minutes, flipping halfway through, until the tofu is golden and slightly crispy.
2. Coat Tofu with BBQ Sauce:
   - Remove the tofu from the oven and transfer it to a mixing bowl.
   - Pour BBQ sauce over the tofu and toss to coat evenly.
3. Assemble Sandwiches:
   - Toast the hamburger buns or sandwich rolls if desired.
   - Place BBQ-coated tofu slices or cubes on the bottom half of each bun.
   - Top with coleslaw, sliced pickles, red onion (if using), and lettuce leaves.
   - Place the top half of the bun over the filling to create sandwiches.
4. Serve:
   - Serve the BBQ tofu sandwiches immediately.

- Enjoy the sandwiches with extra BBQ sauce or your favorite condiments on the side.

Optional Additions and Variations:

- Cheese: Add a slice of vegan cheese or regular cheese to melt over the BBQ tofu.
- Spicy Mayo: Mix vegan mayo with a splash of hot sauce or sriracha for a spicy kick.
- Avocado: Add sliced avocado for creaminess and extra flavor.
- Different Toppings: Customize the sandwiches with your favorite toppings such as sliced tomatoes, jalapeños, or caramelized onions.

These BBQ tofu sandwiches are perfect for lunch or dinner and can be served with a side of potato chips, coleslaw, or a salad. They are easy to make and incredibly delicious! Enjoy this vegetarian twist on a classic BBQ sandwich.

Tofu Tikka Masala

Ingredients:

For Marinated Tofu:

- 14 oz (400g) firm tofu, drained and pressed
- 1 cup plain yogurt (use vegan yogurt for a vegan version)
- 2 tablespoons lemon juice
- 2 tablespoons ginger-garlic paste (or minced ginger and garlic)
- 1 tablespoon ground coriander
- 1 tablespoon ground cumin
- 1 teaspoon turmeric
- 1 teaspoon smoked paprika
- 1/2 teaspoon cayenne pepper (adjust to taste)
- Salt, to taste

For Tikka Masala Sauce:

- 2 tablespoons vegetable oil
- 1 onion, finely chopped
- 3 cloves garlic, minced
- 1 tablespoon grated ginger
- 1 can (14 oz or 400g) crushed tomatoes
- 1 tablespoon tomato paste
- 1 tablespoon ground coriander
- 1 tablespoon ground cumin
- 1 teaspoon turmeric
- 1 teaspoon garam masala
- 1/2 teaspoon smoked paprika
- 1/2 teaspoon cayenne pepper (adjust to taste)
- 1 cup vegetable broth
- 1/2 cup heavy cream or coconut cream (for vegan version)
- Salt and pepper, to taste
- Fresh cilantro, chopped, for garnish
- Cooked rice or naan bread, for serving

Instructions:

1. Prepare Marinated Tofu:
   - Cut the pressed tofu into cubes and set aside.
   - In a mixing bowl, combine yogurt, lemon juice, ginger-garlic paste, ground coriander, ground cumin, turmeric, smoked paprika, cayenne pepper, and salt.
   - Add tofu cubes to the marinade, ensuring they are well coated. Cover and refrigerate for at least 30 minutes (or up to 2 hours) to marinate.
2. Cook Marinated Tofu:
   - Preheat the oven to 400°F (200°C).
   - Arrange marinated tofu cubes on a baking sheet lined with parchment paper.
   - Bake for 20-25 minutes, turning halfway through, until the tofu is golden and slightly crispy. Set aside.
3. Make Tikka Masala Sauce:
   - Heat vegetable oil in a large skillet or pot over medium heat.
   - Add chopped onion and sauté until softened and translucent, about 5-7 minutes.
   - Stir in minced garlic and grated ginger, and cook for another 1-2 minutes until fragrant.
   - Add crushed tomatoes, tomato paste, ground coriander, ground cumin, turmeric, garam masala, smoked paprika, cayenne pepper, salt, and pepper. Mix well to combine.
   - Pour in vegetable broth and simmer for 10-12 minutes, stirring occasionally, until the sauce thickens slightly.
4. Finish the Dish:
   - Stir in heavy cream or coconut cream (for vegan version) into the sauce.
   - Add baked tofu cubes to the sauce and simmer for another 5 minutes to heat through and allow flavors to meld.
   - Taste and adjust seasoning if needed.
5. Serve:
   - Garnish tofu tikka masala with chopped fresh cilantro.
   - Serve hot over cooked rice or with naan bread.
   - Enjoy this flavorful tofu tikka masala as a delicious and comforting meal!

This tofu tikka masala is rich, creamy, and packed with aromatic spices. It's perfect for a special dinner or when you're craving Indian-inspired flavors. Feel free to adjust the level of spiciness to suit your taste preference. Serve with your favorite side dishes and enjoy!

Tofu Satay Skewers

Ingredients:

For Tofu Satay:

- 14 oz (400g) firm tofu, drained and pressed
- 2 tablespoons soy sauce or tamari
- 1 tablespoon sesame oil
- 2 tablespoons lime juice
- 2 tablespoons brown sugar or maple syrup
- 2 cloves garlic, minced
- 1 tablespoon grated ginger
- 1 teaspoon ground turmeric
- 1 teaspoon ground cumin
- Bamboo skewers, soaked in water (if grilling)

For Peanut Dipping Sauce:

- 1/2 cup smooth peanut butter
- 2 tablespoons soy sauce or tamari
- 2 tablespoons maple syrup or honey
- 1 tablespoon rice vinegar
- 1 clove garlic, minced
- 1 tablespoon grated ginger
- Water, as needed to thin the sauce

For Serving:

- Chopped fresh cilantro or parsley, for garnish
- Crushed peanuts, for garnish (optional)
- Cooked rice or noodles, for serving

Instructions:

1. Prepare Tofu Satay:
    - Cut the pressed tofu into cubes or strips suitable for skewering.

- In a bowl, mix together soy sauce (or tamari), sesame oil, lime juice, brown sugar (or maple syrup), minced garlic, grated ginger, ground turmeric, and ground cumin.
- Add tofu cubes/strips to the marinade and toss to coat evenly. Cover and refrigerate for at least 30 minutes (or up to 2 hours) to marinate.

2. Skewer Tofu:
    - If grilling, preheat the grill or grill pan over medium-high heat.
    - Thread marinated tofu cubes/strips onto soaked bamboo skewers.
3. Cook Tofu Satay:
    - Grill the tofu skewers for 3-4 minutes on each side until golden and slightly charred. Alternatively, you can bake the skewers in a preheated oven at 400°F (200°C) for about 20-25 minutes, flipping halfway through.
4. Make Peanut Dipping Sauce:
    - In a small bowl, whisk together peanut butter, soy sauce (or tamari), maple syrup (or honey), rice vinegar, minced garlic, and grated ginger.
    - Gradually add water to thin the sauce to your desired consistency. Mix until smooth and creamy.
5. Serve:
    - Arrange cooked tofu satay skewers on a serving platter.
    - Drizzle peanut dipping sauce over the skewers or serve it on the side for dipping.
    - Garnish with chopped fresh cilantro or parsley and crushed peanuts (if using).
    - Serve hot with cooked rice or noodles.
6. Enjoy:
    - Enjoy these delicious tofu satay skewers with peanut dipping sauce as a flavorful appetizer or main course!

Feel free to customize this recipe by adding chopped vegetables like bell peppers or onions to the skewers before grilling. Serve with a side of salad or steamed vegetables for a complete and satisfying meal. Enjoy!

Tofu Enchiladas

Ingredients:

For Tofu Filling:

- 14 oz (400g) firm tofu, drained and pressed
- 1 tablespoon olive oil
- 1 onion, finely chopped
- 2 cloves garlic, minced
- 1 bell pepper, diced
- 1 teaspoon ground cumin
- 1 teaspoon chili powder
- 1/2 teaspoon smoked paprika
- Salt and pepper, to taste
- 1 can (15 oz) black beans, drained and rinsed
- 1/2 cup corn kernels (fresh, frozen, or canned)

For Enchilada Sauce:

- 2 tablespoons olive oil
- 2 tablespoons all-purpose flour (or use a gluten-free flour blend)
- 3 tablespoons chili powder
- 1 teaspoon ground cumin
- 1/2 teaspoon garlic powder
- 1/4 teaspoon dried oregano
- 2 cups vegetable broth
- Salt and pepper, to taste

For Assembling:

- 8-10 corn tortillas
- 1 cup shredded cheese (cheddar, Monterey Jack, or a dairy-free alternative)
- Chopped fresh cilantro, for garnish
- Sliced jalapeños, for garnish (optional)
- Lime wedges, for serving

Instructions:

1. Prepare Tofu Filling:
   - Preheat the oven to 375°F (190°C).
   - In a skillet, heat olive oil over medium heat. Add chopped onion and cook for 3-4 minutes until translucent.
   - Add minced garlic and diced bell pepper. Cook for another 2-3 minutes until the vegetables are softened.
   - Crumble the pressed tofu into the skillet using your hands or a fork.
   - Stir in ground cumin, chili powder, smoked paprika, salt, and pepper. Cook for 5-6 minutes, stirring occasionally, until tofu is lightly browned and well-coated with spices.
   - Add black beans and corn kernels to the skillet. Stir to combine. Remove from heat and set aside.
2. Prepare Enchilada Sauce:
   - In a saucepan, heat olive oil over medium heat. Whisk in all-purpose flour and cook for 1-2 minutes until lightly golden.
   - Stir in chili powder, ground cumin, garlic powder, and dried oregano. Cook for another minute.
   - Gradually whisk in vegetable broth, stirring constantly to avoid lumps.
   - Bring the sauce to a simmer and cook for 5-7 minutes until thickened. Season with salt and pepper to taste. Remove from heat and set aside.
3. Assemble and Bake Enchiladas:
   - Spread a thin layer of enchilada sauce on the bottom of a baking dish.
   - Warm corn tortillas in the microwave or on a skillet until pliable.
   - Spoon tofu filling onto each tortilla, roll it up, and place it seam-side down in the baking dish.
   - Once all tortillas are filled and arranged in the baking dish, pour the remaining enchilada sauce over the top, covering the tortillas evenly.
   - Sprinkle shredded cheese over the enchiladas.
4. Bake:
   - Cover the baking dish with foil and bake in the preheated oven for 20-25 minutes.
   - Remove the foil and bake for an additional 5-10 minutes until the cheese is melted and bubbly.
5. Serve:
   - Garnish tofu enchiladas with chopped fresh cilantro and sliced jalapeños (if using).
   - Serve hot with lime wedges on the side.

Enjoy these delicious tofu enchiladas as a flavorful and satisfying meal. They are perfect for dinner and can be customized with your favorite toppings and garnishes. Serve with rice, beans, or a side salad for a complete Mexican-inspired feast!

Tofu Scallion Pancakes

Ingredients:

For the Pancake Batter:

- 1 cup all-purpose flour
- 1/2 cup water
- 1/2 cup firm tofu, mashed
- 2 tablespoons soy sauce or tamari
- 2 tablespoons sesame oil
- 2 tablespoons chopped scallions (green onions)
- 1 teaspoon grated ginger
- 1/2 teaspoon salt
- 1/4 teaspoon black pepper
- Vegetable oil, for frying

For Dipping Sauce:

- 3 tablespoons soy sauce or tamari
- 1 tablespoon rice vinegar
- 1 tablespoon sesame oil
- 1 tablespoon chopped scallions (green onions)
- 1 teaspoon grated ginger
- 1 teaspoon honey or maple syrup (optional, for sweetness)

Instructions:

1. Prepare the Pancake Batter:
    - In a mixing bowl, combine all-purpose flour, water, mashed tofu, soy sauce (or tamari), sesame oil, chopped scallions, grated ginger, salt, and black pepper.
    - Mix until a smooth batter forms. The batter should be thick but pourable.
2. Cook the Pancakes:
    - Heat a non-stick skillet or frying pan over medium heat.
    - Add a small amount of vegetable oil to the skillet, just enough to coat the bottom.
    - Pour a ladleful of pancake batter into the skillet, spreading it out to form a round pancake (about 6 inches in diameter).

- Cook for 2-3 minutes on each side until golden brown and crispy. Repeat with the remaining batter, adding more oil to the skillet as needed.
3. Make the Dipping Sauce:
    - In a small bowl, whisk together soy sauce (or tamari), rice vinegar, sesame oil, chopped scallions, grated ginger, and honey or maple syrup (if using).
    - Adjust seasoning to taste by adding more soy sauce, vinegar, or sweetener as desired.
4. Serve:
    - Cut the tofu scallion pancakes into wedges or squares.
    - Serve hot with the dipping sauce on the side.
    - Enjoy the crispy and savory tofu scallion pancakes as a delicious appetizer or snack!

These tofu scallion pancakes are packed with flavor and make a wonderful addition to any meal. They are crispy on the outside, tender on the inside, and perfectly complemented by the tangy dipping sauce. Feel free to customize the recipe by adding other vegetables or spices to the pancake batter. Enjoy!

Tofu Frittata

Ingredients:

- 14 oz (400g) firm tofu, drained and pressed
- 1 tablespoon olive oil
- 1 onion, diced
- 2 garlic cloves, minced
- 1 bell pepper, diced
- 1 cup mushrooms, sliced
- 1 cup spinach leaves, chopped
- 1/4 cup nutritional yeast (for cheesy flavor)
- 1 teaspoon ground turmeric
- 1/2 teaspoon ground cumin
- Salt and pepper, to taste
- Optional additions: diced tomatoes, chopped broccoli, vegan cheese

Instructions:

1. Prepare the Tofu:
    - Drain the tofu and press it to remove excess moisture. You can do this by wrapping the tofu block in paper towels and placing something heavy on top for about 15-20 minutes.
2. Cook the Vegetables:
    - Preheat the oven to 375°F (190°C).
    - In an oven-safe skillet, heat olive oil over medium heat.
    - Add diced onion and garlic, sauté for 2-3 minutes until translucent.
    - Add diced bell pepper and sliced mushrooms. Cook for another 5-7 minutes until vegetables are tender.
    - Add chopped spinach and cook until wilted. Season with salt and pepper.
3. Prepare the Tofu Mixture:
    - In a bowl, crumble the pressed tofu using your hands or a fork.
    - Add nutritional yeast, ground turmeric, ground cumin, salt, and pepper to the crumbled tofu. Mix well to combine.
4. Combine and Bake:
    - Add the seasoned tofu mixture to the skillet with the cooked vegetables. Mix everything together until well combined.
    - Flatten the mixture with a spatula to evenly distribute in the skillet.
    - Optionally, sprinkle diced tomatoes, chopped broccoli, or vegan cheese on top.

5. Bake the Frittata:
   - Transfer the skillet to the preheated oven.
   - Bake for 25-30 minutes until the frittata is set and the edges are golden brown.
6. Serve:
   - Remove the tofu frittata from the oven and let it cool slightly.
   - Slice into wedges and serve hot.
   - Enjoy your delicious tofu frittata as a hearty and satisfying breakfast, brunch, or lunch!

This tofu frittata is versatile, healthy, and packed with plant-based protein and nutrients.

Feel free to customize the recipe by adding your favorite vegetables, herbs, or spices.

Serve with a side salad, toast, or roasted potatoes for a complete meal. Enjoy!

Tofu and Kale Salad with Sesame Dressing

Ingredients:

For the Salad:

- 14 oz (400g) firm tofu, drained and pressed
- 1 bunch kale, stems removed and leaves chopped
- 1 carrot, grated
- 1 cucumber, thinly sliced
- 1/4 cup chopped cilantro or parsley
- 2 tablespoons sesame seeds, toasted

For the Sesame Dressing:

- 3 tablespoons soy sauce or tamari
- 2 tablespoons rice vinegar
- 1 tablespoon sesame oil
- 1 tablespoon maple syrup or honey
- 1 clove garlic, minced
- 1 teaspoon grated ginger
- 1 tablespoon water (optional, to thin the dressing)

Instructions:

1. Prepare the Tofu:
    - Cut the pressed tofu into cubes or slices.
    - In a non-stick skillet or frying pan, heat a small amount of oil over medium-high heat.
    - Add the tofu cubes/slices and cook for 3-4 minutes on each side until golden and crispy. Set aside.
2. Prepare the Kale:
    - Place the chopped kale in a large salad bowl.
    - Massage the kale with your hands for a few minutes to soften it and make it more tender.
3. Assemble the Salad:
    - Add grated carrot, sliced cucumber, chopped cilantro (or parsley), and toasted sesame seeds to the bowl with the kale.
    - Add the cooked tofu to the salad.
4. Make the Sesame Dressing:

- In a small bowl, whisk together soy sauce (or tamari), rice vinegar, sesame oil, maple syrup (or honey), minced garlic, and grated ginger.
- If the dressing is too strong or thick, you can add a tablespoon of water to thin it out.

5. Combine and Serve:
   - Pour the sesame dressing over the salad ingredients.
   - Toss everything together until well coated with the dressing.
   - Serve the tofu and kale salad immediately, garnished with additional sesame seeds if desired.

This tofu and kale salad with sesame dressing is nutritious, flavorful, and packed with plant-based protein and vitamins. It's perfect for a light lunch or dinner, and you can easily customize it by adding other vegetables or toppings. Enjoy this healthy and delicious salad!

Tofu Banh Mi Sandwiches

Ingredients:

For Marinated Tofu:

- 14 oz (400g) firm tofu, drained and pressed
- 2 tablespoons soy sauce or tamari
- 2 tablespoons rice vinegar
- 1 tablespoon sesame oil
- 1 tablespoon maple syrup or honey
- 2 cloves garlic, minced
- 1 teaspoon grated ginger
- Salt and pepper, to taste

For Pickled Vegetables:

- 1 medium carrot, julienned or thinly sliced
- 1/2 daikon radish, julienned or thinly sliced
- 1/4 cup rice vinegar
- 1 tablespoon sugar
- 1/2 teaspoon salt

For Sandwich Assembly:

- Baguette or sandwich rolls, sliced lengthwise
- Vegan mayonnaise or sriracha mayo
- Fresh cilantro sprigs
- Fresh mint leaves
- Sliced cucumber
- Sliced jalapeño peppers (optional)

For Sauce (optional):

- 2 tablespoons soy sauce or tamari
- 2 tablespoons hoisin sauce
- 1 tablespoon Sriracha sauce (adjust to taste)
- 1 tablespoon lime juice

Instructions:

1. Prepare Marinated Tofu:
   - Cut the pressed tofu into thin slices or strips.
   - In a bowl, whisk together soy sauce (or tamari), rice vinegar, sesame oil, maple syrup (or honey), minced garlic, grated ginger, salt, and pepper.
   - Add tofu slices/strips to the marinade and let marinate for at least 30 minutes (or up to 2 hours) in the refrigerator.
2. Prepare Pickled Vegetables:
   - In a bowl, combine julienned carrot and daikon radish.
   - In a separate bowl, mix rice vinegar, sugar, and salt until dissolved.
   - Pour the vinegar mixture over the vegetables and toss to coat. Let it sit for at least 30 minutes to pickle.
3. Cook Tofu:
   - Heat a non-stick skillet or grill pan over medium-high heat.
   - Cook marinated tofu slices/strips for 3-4 minutes on each side until golden and crispy. Set aside.
4. Assemble Banh Mi Sandwiches:
   - Slice the baguette or sandwich rolls lengthwise.
   - Spread vegan mayonnaise or sriracha mayo on the bottom half of the bread.
   - Layer with cooked tofu slices/strips.
   - Top with pickled vegetables, sliced cucumber, fresh cilantro sprigs, mint leaves, and sliced jalapeños (if using).
5. Optional Sauce:
   - In a small bowl, whisk together soy sauce (or tamari), hoisin sauce, Sriracha sauce, and lime juice to make a tangy sauce.
   - Drizzle the sauce over the assembled banh mi sandwiches.
6. Serve:
   - Close the sandwiches with the top half of the baguette or sandwich rolls.
   - Slice the sandwiches in half if desired.
   - Serve tofu banh mi sandwiches immediately and enjoy the delicious flavors!

These tofu banh mi sandwiches are bursting with flavor, texture, and freshness. They make a perfect lunch or dinner option and are great for picnics or gatherings. Feel free to customize the sandwiches with your favorite toppings and adjust the spice level according to your taste. Enjoy!

Tofu Mushroom Pot Pie

Ingredients:

For the Filling:

- 14 oz (400g) firm tofu, drained and pressed
- 2 tablespoons olive oil
- 1 onion, chopped
- 2 cloves garlic, minced
- 8 oz (225g) mushrooms, sliced (cremini or button mushrooms work well)
- 1 carrot, diced
- 1 celery stalk, diced
- 1 teaspoon dried thyme
- 1 teaspoon dried rosemary
- Salt and pepper, to taste
- 2 tablespoons all-purpose flour
- 1 cup vegetable broth
- 1 cup frozen peas
- 1/2 cup unsweetened non-dairy milk (such as almond milk or oat milk)
- Fresh parsley, chopped (for garnish)

For the Pie Crust:

- 1 package (2 sheets) store-bought puff pastry (vegan-friendly)
- 1 tablespoon non-dairy milk, for brushing

Instructions:

1. Prepare the Filling:
    - Preheat the oven to 400°F (200°C).
    - Cut the pressed tofu into cubes.
    - In a large skillet, heat olive oil over medium heat.
    - Add chopped onion and garlic, and sauté until softened, about 3-4 minutes.
    - Add sliced mushrooms, diced carrot, and diced celery to the skillet. Cook for another 5-6 minutes until mushrooms release their moisture and begin to brown.
    - Stir in dried thyme, dried rosemary, salt, and pepper.
2. Make the Sauce:

- Sprinkle all-purpose flour over the vegetables in the skillet. Stir well to coat evenly.
- Gradually pour in vegetable broth and non-dairy milk, stirring constantly to prevent lumps.
- Cook for 2-3 minutes until the sauce thickens and becomes creamy.
- Add frozen peas and cubed tofu to the skillet. Mix well to combine. Remove from heat.

3. Assemble the Pot Pie:
   - Transfer the tofu mushroom filling to a deep pie dish or oven-safe casserole dish.
   - Roll out the puff pastry sheets on a lightly floured surface to fit over the dish.
   - Place the rolled-out pastry sheet over the filling, trimming any excess pastry hanging over the edges.
   - Crimp or press the edges of the pastry to seal the dish.
   - Brush the top of the pastry with non-dairy milk for a golden finish.

4. Bake the Pot Pie:
   - Place the assembled pot pie in the preheated oven.
   - Bake for 25-30 minutes or until the pastry is golden brown and the filling is bubbling.
   - If the pastry browns too quickly, cover the pot pie with foil halfway through baking.

5. Serve:
   - Remove the tofu mushroom pot pie from the oven and let it cool slightly.
   - Garnish with chopped fresh parsley.
   - Slice and serve warm.

Enjoy this delicious tofu mushroom pot pie as a comforting and satisfying meal. It's perfect for dinner gatherings and can be served with a side salad or steamed vegetables. Feel free to customize the filling with your favorite herbs and vegetables. Enjoy!

Tofu BLT Wraps

Ingredients:

- 14 oz (400g) firm tofu, drained and pressed
- 2 tablespoons soy sauce or tamari
- 1 tablespoon maple syrup or agave nectar
- 1 teaspoon smoked paprika
- 1/2 teaspoon garlic powder
- 1/4 teaspoon black pepper
- 1 tablespoon olive oil
- 4 large flour tortillas or wraps
- Vegan mayonnaise or tahini, for spreading
- Lettuce leaves (romaine or green leaf)
- Sliced tomatoes
- Sliced avocado
- Cooked vegan bacon strips (optional, for added flavor)
- Salt and pepper, to taste

Instructions:

1. Prepare the Tofu:
    - Cut the pressed tofu into thin slices or strips.
    - In a shallow dish, whisk together soy sauce (or tamari), maple syrup (or agave nectar), smoked paprika, garlic powder, and black pepper.
    - Add tofu slices/strips to the marinade and let marinate for at least 15-20 minutes.
2. Cook the Tofu:
    - Heat olive oil in a non-stick skillet or frying pan over medium-high heat.
    - Add the marinated tofu slices/strips to the skillet.
    - Cook for 3-4 minutes on each side until golden brown and crispy. Remove from heat and set aside.
3. Assemble the Wraps:
    - Lay a tortilla or wrap flat on a clean surface.
    - Spread a layer of vegan mayonnaise or tahini over the tortilla.
    - Arrange lettuce leaves, sliced tomatoes, and sliced avocado on top of the spread.
    - Place cooked tofu slices/strips and vegan bacon strips (if using) over the vegetables.
    - Season with salt and pepper, if desired.

4. Roll the Wraps:
   - Fold the sides of the tortilla inward, then roll it up tightly from the bottom to enclose the filling.
   - Repeat with the remaining tortillas and filling ingredients.
5. Serve and Enjoy:
   - Slice the tofu BLT wraps in half diagonally, if desired.
   - Serve immediately and enjoy these delicious and satisfying wraps!

These tofu BLT wraps are perfect for a quick lunch or dinner, and they can be customized with your favorite toppings and condiments. Feel free to add extras like pickles, sprouts, or roasted vegetables to make them your own. Enjoy the flavors and textures of this plant-based twist on a classic sandwich!

Tofu Ratatouille

Ingredients:

- 14 oz (400g) firm tofu, drained and pressed
- 2 tablespoons olive oil
- 1 onion, diced
- 2 cloves garlic, minced
- 1 eggplant, diced
- 2 zucchini, diced
- 1 bell pepper (red, yellow, or green), diced
- 2 cups diced tomatoes (canned or fresh)
- 1 tablespoon tomato paste
- 1 teaspoon dried thyme
- 1 teaspoon dried basil
- Salt and pepper, to taste
- Fresh basil or parsley, chopped (for garnish)

Instructions:

1. Prepare the Tofu:
    - Cut the pressed tofu into cubes or strips.
2. Cook the Vegetables:
    - In a large skillet or pot, heat olive oil over medium heat.
    - Add diced onion and garlic, and sauté until softened and fragrant, about 3-4 minutes.
    - Add diced eggplant, zucchini, and bell pepper to the skillet. Cook for another 5-7 minutes until the vegetables start to soften.
3. Add Tomatoes and Seasonings:
    - Stir in diced tomatoes, tomato paste, dried thyme, and dried basil.
    - Season with salt and pepper to taste.
    - Bring the mixture to a simmer, then reduce the heat to low. Cover and let it simmer for about 15-20 minutes, stirring occasionally, until the vegetables are tender and the flavors meld together.
4. Add Tofu and Finish Cooking:
    - Gently add the tofu cubes or strips to the vegetable mixture.
    - Stir to combine and simmer for an additional 5 minutes to heat the tofu through.
5. Serve:
    - Remove from heat and garnish with chopped fresh basil or parsley.

- Serve the tofu ratatouille hot as a main dish, either on its own or with crusty bread, rice, or pasta.

Enjoy this delicious and nutritious tofu ratatouille, which is packed with vegetables and flavor. It's a perfect dish for showcasing seasonal produce and makes a satisfying meal for vegetarians and vegans alike. Bon appétit!

Tofu and Corn Chowder

Ingredients:

- 14 oz (400g) firm tofu, drained and pressed
- 2 tablespoons olive oil
- 1 onion, diced
- 2 cloves garlic, minced
- 2 stalks celery, diced
- 2 carrots, diced
- 1 red bell pepper, diced
- 2 potatoes, peeled and diced
- 1 can (15 oz) sweet corn kernels, drained (or use fresh corn kernels)
- 4 cups vegetable broth
- 1 cup unsweetened non-dairy milk (such as almond milk or oat milk)
- 2 tablespoons all-purpose flour (or use a gluten-free flour blend)
- 1 teaspoon dried thyme
- 1 teaspoon dried oregano
- Salt and pepper, to taste
- Fresh parsley or chives, chopped (for garnish)

Instructions:

1. Prepare the Tofu:
    - Cut the pressed tofu into small cubes.
2. Cook the Vegetables:
    - In a large pot, heat olive oil over medium heat.
    - Add diced onion, garlic, celery, carrots, and red bell pepper. Sauté for 5-7 minutes until vegetables start to soften.
3. Add Potatoes and Corn:
    - Add diced potatoes and drained corn kernels to the pot.
    - Stir to combine with the vegetables.
4. Make the Chowder Base:
    - Sprinkle all-purpose flour over the vegetables in the pot. Stir well to coat.
    - Gradually pour in vegetable broth and non-dairy milk, stirring constantly to prevent lumps.
    - Add dried thyme, dried oregano, salt, and pepper to taste.
    - Bring the mixture to a simmer, then reduce the heat to low. Cover and let it simmer for about 15-20 minutes until the potatoes are tender and the soup thickens.

5. Add Tofu and Finish Cooking:
    - Gently add the tofu cubes to the soup.
    - Simmer for an additional 5 minutes to heat the tofu through and blend the flavors.
6. Serve:
    - Remove from heat and adjust seasoning if needed.
    - Ladle the tofu and corn chowder into bowls.
    - Garnish with chopped fresh parsley or chives.
    - Serve hot and enjoy this creamy and flavorful soup!

Feel free to customize this tofu and corn chowder by adding other vegetables or herbs according to your preference. Serve with crusty bread or crackers for a satisfying meal. This soup is perfect for lunch or dinner and can be easily reheated for leftovers. Enjoy!

Tofu Katsu

Ingredients:

For Tofu Katsu:

- 14 oz (400g) firm tofu, drained and pressed
- 1 cup panko breadcrumbs (use gluten-free panko for a gluten-free option)
- 1/4 cup all-purpose flour (or use cornstarch for a gluten-free option)
- 1/2 cup plant-based milk (such as soy milk or almond milk)
- 1 tablespoon soy sauce or tamari
- 1 tablespoon vegetable oil, for frying
- Salt and pepper, to taste

For Tonkatsu Sauce (Dipping Sauce):

- 3 tablespoons ketchup
- 2 tablespoons soy sauce or tamari
- 1 tablespoon Worcestershire sauce (use vegan Worcestershire sauce if preferred)
- 1 tablespoon maple syrup or sugar
- 1 teaspoon Dijon mustard (optional)

For Serving:

- Cooked rice
- Shredded cabbage (optional)
- Lemon wedges (for garnish)

Instructions:

1. Prepare the Tofu:
    - Cut the pressed tofu into thick slices (about 1/2 inch thick).
    - Season the tofu slices with salt and pepper on both sides.
2. Coat the Tofu:
    - Prepare three shallow bowls: one with all-purpose flour (or cornstarch), one with plant-based milk mixed with soy sauce (or tamari), and one with panko breadcrumbs.
    - Dip each tofu slice into the flour, then into the milk mixture, and finally into the panko breadcrumbs, pressing gently to coat evenly.

3. Fry the Tofu:
   - In a large skillet, heat vegetable oil over medium-high heat.
   - Carefully place the breaded tofu slices in the skillet.
   - Fry for about 3-4 minutes on each side, or until golden and crispy.
   - Remove the tofu slices from the skillet and place them on a paper towel-lined plate to drain excess oil.
4. Make Tonkatsu Sauce (Dipping Sauce):
   - In a small bowl, whisk together ketchup, soy sauce (or tamari), Worcestershire sauce, maple syrup (or sugar), and Dijon mustard (if using).
   - Adjust the seasoning according to your taste.
5. Serve Tofu Katsu:
   - Slice the crispy tofu katsu into strips.
   - Serve hot with cooked rice, shredded cabbage (if using), and tonkatsu sauce on the side.
   - Garnish with lemon wedges for a fresh touch.

Enjoy this delicious tofu katsu with its crispy texture and savory flavor! It's a fantastic dish for lunch or dinner, and it pairs perfectly with the tangy tonkatsu sauce and fluffy rice. Feel free to customize by adding your favorite sides or vegetables. Enjoy!

Tofu Stroganoff

Ingredients:

- 14 oz (400g) firm tofu, drained and pressed
- 8 oz (225g) cremini mushrooms, sliced
- 1 onion, finely chopped
- 2 cloves garlic, minced
- 2 tablespoons olive oil or vegan butter
- 1 tablespoon all-purpose flour (or use a gluten-free flour blend)
- 1 cup vegetable broth
- 1 cup unsweetened non-dairy milk (such as almond milk or oat milk)
- 2 tablespoons soy sauce or tamari
- 1 tablespoon Dijon mustard
- 1 tablespoon tomato paste
- 1 teaspoon paprika
- Salt and pepper, to taste
- Cooked egg noodles, rice, or mashed potatoes, for serving
- Chopped fresh parsley or chives, for garnish

Instructions:

1. Prepare the Tofu:
    - Cut the pressed tofu into cubes or strips.
2. Cook the Tofu and Mushrooms:
    - In a large skillet, heat olive oil or vegan butter over medium-high heat.
    - Add the tofu cubes to the skillet and cook for 5-7 minutes, turning occasionally, until golden and crispy. Remove tofu from the skillet and set aside.
    - In the same skillet, add sliced mushrooms and cook for 5-6 minutes until mushrooms release their moisture and start to brown. Remove mushrooms from the skillet and set aside.
3. Make the Sauce:
    - In the same skillet, add chopped onion and garlic. Sauté for 3-4 minutes until softened.
    - Sprinkle all-purpose flour over the onion and garlic, stirring to coat.
    - Gradually pour in vegetable broth and non-dairy milk, stirring constantly to prevent lumps.
    - Stir in soy sauce (or tamari), Dijon mustard, tomato paste, paprika, salt, and pepper.

- Bring the mixture to a simmer, then reduce heat to low. Cook for 5-7 minutes until the sauce thickens.
4. Combine and Serve:
    - Add the cooked tofu and mushrooms back into the skillet with the sauce. Stir to combine and heat through.
    - Taste and adjust seasoning if needed.
    - Serve the tofu stroganoff hot over cooked egg noodles, rice, or mashed potatoes.
    - Garnish with chopped fresh parsley or chives.

Enjoy this creamy and comforting tofu stroganoff as a satisfying main dish. It's perfect for a cozy dinner and is sure to be a hit with vegetarians and vegans alike. Feel free to customize the recipe with your favorite herbs and spices. Enjoy!

Tofu Tikki Burger

Ingredients:

For Tofu Patties:

- 14 oz (400g) firm tofu, drained and pressed
- 1/2 cup bread crumbs (use gluten-free bread crumbs if needed)
- 1/4 cup finely chopped onion
- 2 cloves garlic, minced
- 1 teaspoon grated ginger
- 1 teaspoon ground cumin
- 1 teaspoon ground coriander
- 1/2 teaspoon turmeric powder
- 1/2 teaspoon chili powder (adjust to taste)
- 2 tablespoons chopped fresh cilantro (coriander leaves)
- Salt and pepper, to taste
- 2 tablespoons oil, for frying

For Burger Assembly:

- Burger buns, toasted
- Lettuce leaves
- Sliced tomatoes
- Sliced onions
- Pickles
- Vegan mayo or your favorite burger sauce

Instructions:

1. Prepare the Tofu Mixture:
    - In a mixing bowl, crumble the pressed tofu using your hands or a fork.
    - Add bread crumbs, finely chopped onion, minced garlic, grated ginger, ground cumin, ground coriander, turmeric powder, chili powder, chopped cilantro, salt, and pepper.
    - Mix well until all ingredients are combined and the mixture holds together.
2. Shape the Tofu Patties:
    - Divide the tofu mixture into 4-6 portions (depending on the size of your burger buns).

- Shape each portion into a round patty using your hands. Press firmly to compact the mixture.

3. Cook the Tofu Patties:
   - Heat oil in a non-stick skillet or frying pan over medium heat.
   - Place the tofu patties in the skillet and cook for 4-5 minutes on each side, or until golden brown and crispy.
   - Use a spatula to carefully flip the patties to prevent them from breaking apart.
4. Assemble the Tofu Tikki Burgers:
   - Toast the burger buns until lightly browned.
   - Spread vegan mayo or your favorite burger sauce on the bottom half of each bun.
   - Place a lettuce leaf on top of the sauce.
   - Add a tofu patty on top of the lettuce.
   - Layer with sliced tomatoes, sliced onions, and pickles.
   - Top with the other half of the burger bun.
5. Serve and Enjoy:
   - Serve the tofu tikki burgers immediately while warm.
   - Enjoy these delicious and flavorful burgers with your favorite side dishes or fries.

Feel free to customize your tofu tikki burgers with additional toppings such as avocado slices, vegan cheese, or caramelized onions. This recipe is versatile and can be adjusted based on your preferences. Enjoy your homemade tofu tikki burgers!

Tofu Thai Green Curry

Ingredients:

- 14 oz (400g) firm tofu, drained and pressed
- 2 tablespoons vegetable oil
- 1 onion, sliced
- 2 bell peppers (any color), sliced
- 1 zucchini, sliced
- 1 cup sliced mushrooms (such as button or cremini)
- 1 can (14 oz) coconut milk
- 2 tablespoons Thai green curry paste (adjust based on preferred spice level)
- 1 tablespoon soy sauce or tamari
- 1 tablespoon brown sugar or coconut sugar
- 1 cup baby spinach leaves (or use other leafy greens like kale)
- Fresh basil or cilantro leaves, for garnish
- Cooked jasmine rice or noodles, for serving

Instructions:

1. Prepare the Tofu:
    - Cut the pressed tofu into cubes.
2. Cook the Vegetables:
    - Heat vegetable oil in a large skillet or pot over medium heat.
    - Add sliced onion and sauté for 2-3 minutes until softened.
    - Add sliced bell peppers, zucchini, and mushrooms to the skillet. Cook for another 5 minutes until vegetables are tender-crisp.
3. Make the Green Curry Sauce:
    - Push the vegetables to one side of the skillet and add the tofu cubes to the empty space.
    - Cook the tofu for 3-4 minutes until lightly browned on all sides.
    - In the same skillet, add Thai green curry paste and stir to coat the vegetables and tofu.
    - Pour in the coconut milk, soy sauce (or tamari), and brown sugar (or coconut sugar). Stir well to combine and bring to a simmer.
4. Simmer the Curry:
    - Reduce the heat to low and let the curry simmer for 8-10 minutes, stirring occasionally, to allow the flavors to meld together and the sauce to thicken slightly.
5. Add Leafy Greens:

- Add baby spinach leaves (or other leafy greens) to the curry. Stir until wilted.
6. Serve the Tofu Thai Green Curry:
    - Remove from heat and taste the curry. Adjust seasoning with more soy sauce, sugar, or curry paste if desired.
    - Serve the tofu Thai green curry hot over cooked jasmine rice or noodles.
    - Garnish with fresh basil or cilantro leaves.

Enjoy this flavorful and aromatic tofu Thai green curry as a satisfying and nourishing meal. Customize the vegetables based on your preference and add extra garnishes or toppings such as crushed peanuts or lime wedges for extra flavor. This dish is perfect for a cozy dinner and will surely impress your taste buds with its Thai-inspired flavors!

Tofu and Black Bean Tacos

Ingredients:

- 14 oz (400g) firm tofu, drained and pressed
- 1 tablespoon olive oil
- 1 onion, diced
- 2 cloves garlic, minced
- 1 bell pepper (any color), diced
- 1 can (15 oz) black beans, drained and rinsed
- 1 tablespoon chili powder
- 1 teaspoon ground cumin
- 1/2 teaspoon smoked paprika
- Salt and pepper, to taste
- Juice of 1 lime
- Small tortillas (corn or flour), for serving
- Toppings: chopped fresh cilantro, sliced avocado, shredded lettuce, diced tomatoes, salsa, sour cream or vegan sour cream, lime wedges

Instructions:

1. Prepare the Tofu:
   - Crumble the pressed tofu into small pieces using your hands or a fork.
2. Cook the Tofu and Vegetables:
   - Heat olive oil in a large skillet over medium heat.
   - Add diced onion and minced garlic. Sauté for 2-3 minutes until onion is translucent.
   - Add diced bell pepper to the skillet and cook for another 2-3 minutes until softened.
   - Push the vegetables to the side of the skillet and add the crumbled tofu to the empty space.
   - Cook the tofu for 5-6 minutes, stirring occasionally, until it starts to brown and crisp up.
3. Add Black Beans and Seasonings:
   - Stir in drained and rinsed black beans into the skillet with the tofu and vegetables.
   - Add chili powder, ground cumin, smoked paprika, salt, and pepper. Stir to combine.
   - Squeeze the juice of 1 lime over the mixture and stir again.
4. Assemble the Tacos:

- Warm the tortillas in a dry skillet or microwave.
- Spoon the tofu and black bean mixture onto each tortilla.
- Top with chopped fresh cilantro, sliced avocado, shredded lettuce, diced tomatoes, salsa, and a dollop of sour cream or vegan sour cream.
- Serve with lime wedges on the side.

5. Enjoy Your Tofu and Black Bean Tacos:
    - Roll up the tacos and enjoy them immediately.
    - Serve with additional toppings or sides as desired.

These tofu and black bean tacos are versatile and can be customized with your favorite toppings and seasonings. They make a fantastic meal for lunch or dinner, and they're perfect for Taco Tuesday or any day of the week! Enjoy the delicious flavors and textures of these vegetarian tacos.

Tofu and Chickpea Tagine

Ingredients:

- 14 oz (400g) firm tofu, drained and pressed
- 1 can (15 oz) chickpeas (garbanzo beans), drained and rinsed
- 2 tablespoons olive oil
- 1 onion, finely chopped
- 3 cloves garlic, minced
- 1 teaspoon ground cumin
- 1 teaspoon ground coriander
- 1 teaspoon ground turmeric
- 1/2 teaspoon ground cinnamon
- 1/4 teaspoon cayenne pepper (adjust to taste)
- 1 can (14 oz) diced tomatoes
- 1 cup vegetable broth
- 2 tablespoons tomato paste
- 1 tablespoon honey or maple syrup
- Salt and pepper, to taste
- Zest of 1 lemon
- Fresh cilantro (coriander) or parsley, chopped, for garnish
- Cooked couscous or rice, for serving

Instructions:

1. Prepare the Tofu:
    - Cut the pressed tofu into cubes.
2. Cook the Tofu:
    - Heat 1 tablespoon of olive oil in a large skillet or Dutch oven over medium-high heat.
    - Add the tofu cubes and cook for 5-7 minutes, turning occasionally, until golden and crispy on all sides.
    - Remove the tofu from the skillet and set aside.
3. Make the Tagine Sauce:
    - In the same skillet, add the remaining tablespoon of olive oil.
    - Add chopped onion and minced garlic. Sauté for 3-4 minutes until softened.
    - Add ground cumin, ground coriander, ground turmeric, ground cinnamon, and cayenne pepper. Stir and cook for 1 minute until fragrant.
4. Simmer the Tagine:

- Stir in diced tomatoes, vegetable broth, and tomato paste into the skillet.
- Add honey or maple syrup, and season with salt and pepper to taste.
- Bring the mixture to a simmer, then reduce heat to low and cover. Let it simmer for 10 minutes to allow the flavors to meld.

5. Add Tofu and Chickpeas:
   - Gently stir in the cooked tofu cubes and drained chickpeas into the tagine sauce.
   - Continue to simmer for another 5-7 minutes until heated through and the sauce thickens slightly.
6. Finish and Serve:
   - Stir in lemon zest and chopped fresh cilantro or parsley.
   - Taste and adjust seasoning if needed.
   - Serve the tofu and chickpea tagine hot over cooked couscous or rice.
   - Garnish with additional fresh herbs if desired.

Enjoy this delicious and comforting tofu and chickpea tagine with its aromatic spices and rich sauce. It's a satisfying vegetarian dish that's perfect for a cozy dinner. Feel free to customize the spices and adjust the sweetness to your liking. Bon appétit!

Tofu Scampi

Ingredients:

- 14 oz (400g) firm tofu, drained and pressed
- 8 oz (225g) linguine or spaghetti
- 4 tablespoons butter (use vegan butter for a vegan option)
- 4 tablespoons olive oil
- 4 cloves garlic, minced
- Zest and juice of 1 lemon
- 1/4 cup dry white wine (optional)
- Salt and pepper, to taste
- Crushed red pepper flakes, to taste (optional)
- Chopped fresh parsley, for garnish

Instructions:

1. Prepare the Tofu:
    - Cut the pressed tofu into cubes or strips.
2. Cook the Pasta:
    - Cook the linguine or spaghetti according to package instructions until al dente. Drain and set aside.
3. Cook the Tofu:
    - In a large skillet, heat 2 tablespoons of butter and 2 tablespoons of olive oil over medium-high heat.
    - Add the tofu cubes to the skillet and cook for 4-5 minutes, turning occasionally, until golden and crispy on all sides.
    - Remove the tofu from the skillet and set aside.
4. Make the Scampi Sauce:
    - In the same skillet, add the remaining 2 tablespoons of butter and 2 tablespoons of olive oil.
    - Add minced garlic and sauté for 1-2 minutes until fragrant.
    - Pour in the white wine (if using) and simmer for 1 minute to reduce slightly.
    - Stir in the lemon zest and juice. Season with salt, pepper, and crushed red pepper flakes (if using).
5. Combine and Serve:
    - Add the cooked tofu and drained pasta to the skillet with the scampi sauce.
    - Toss everything together gently to coat the pasta and tofu with the sauce.

- Cook for an additional minute to heat through.
6. Garnish and Enjoy:
    - Remove from heat and garnish with chopped fresh parsley.
    - Serve the tofu scampi hot, with additional lemon wedges or grated Parmesan cheese (use vegan Parmesan if preferred) if desired.

Enjoy this delicious and flavorful tofu scampi as a satisfying vegetarian meal. The combination of garlic, lemon, and crispy tofu creates a wonderful dish that's perfect for pasta lovers. Feel free to customize the dish with your favorite herbs or additional vegetables. Bon appétit!

Tofu and Avocado Quesadillas

Ingredients:

- 14 oz (400g) firm tofu, drained and pressed
- 1 ripe avocado, sliced
- 1 cup shredded cheese (cheddar, Monterey Jack, or vegan cheese)
- 4 large flour tortillas
- 2 tablespoons olive oil
- 1 teaspoon chili powder
- 1/2 teaspoon ground cumin
- 1/2 teaspoon garlic powder
- Salt and pepper, to taste
- Salsa, sour cream (or vegan sour cream), or guacamole, for serving

Instructions:

1. Prepare the Tofu:
    - Cut the pressed tofu into thin slices or cubes.
2. Season and Cook the Tofu:
    - In a bowl, combine the tofu slices or cubes with chili powder, ground cumin, garlic powder, salt, and pepper. Toss well to coat.
    - Heat olive oil in a skillet over medium heat.
    - Add the seasoned tofu to the skillet and cook for 4-5 minutes, stirring occasionally, until golden and crispy. Remove from heat and set aside.
3. Assemble the Quesadillas:
    - Lay out one tortilla on a flat surface.
    - Sprinkle a quarter of the shredded cheese evenly over half of the tortilla.
    - Arrange a quarter of the cooked tofu and sliced avocado on top of the cheese.
    - Fold the tortilla in half over the filling to create a half-moon shape.
4. Cook the Quesadillas:
    - Heat a clean skillet or griddle over medium heat.
    - Carefully transfer the assembled quesadilla to the hot skillet.
    - Cook for 2-3 minutes on each side, or until the tortilla is golden and crispy and the cheese is melted.
    - Repeat with the remaining tortillas and filling ingredients.
5. Serve and Enjoy:
    - Once cooked, remove the quesadillas from the skillet and let them cool for a minute.

- Cut each quesadilla into wedges using a sharp knife or pizza cutter.
- Serve hot with salsa, sour cream (or vegan sour cream), or guacamole on the side for dipping.

These tofu and avocado quesadillas are perfect for a quick and delicious meal. They can be customized with additional toppings such as diced tomatoes, chopped cilantro, or jalapeños. Enjoy these flavorful quesadillas for lunch, dinner, or as a tasty snack!

Tofu Chive Dumplings

Ingredients:

For the Dumpling Filling:

- 14 oz (400g) firm tofu, drained and pressed
- 1 cup chopped chives (Chinese chives or garlic chives are preferred)
- 2 cloves garlic, minced
- 1 tablespoon soy sauce
- 1 tablespoon sesame oil
- 1 teaspoon grated ginger
- 1/2 teaspoon salt
- 1/4 teaspoon white pepper
- Optional: 1 tablespoon cornstarch (to help bind the filling)

For the Dumpling Wrappers:

- Dumpling wrappers (store-bought or homemade)

For Dipping Sauce (Optional):

- 2 tablespoons soy sauce
- 1 tablespoon rice vinegar
- 1 teaspoon sesame oil
- Optional: chopped green onions or chili oil for heat

Instructions:

1. Prepare the Dumpling Filling:
    - In a mixing bowl, crumble the pressed tofu using your hands or a fork.
    - Add chopped chives, minced garlic, soy sauce, sesame oil, grated ginger, salt, and white pepper to the crumbled tofu.
    - Mix well to combine all ingredients. If the mixture feels too wet, you can add a tablespoon of cornstarch to help bind the filling.
2. Assemble the Dumplings:
    - Place a small spoonful of the tofu and chive filling onto the center of a dumpling wrapper.
    - Moisten the edges of the wrapper with water.
    - Fold the wrapper in half over the filling to create a half-moon shape.
    - Press the edges together firmly to seal the dumpling. You can crimp the edges or pleat them for a decorative look.

3. Cook the Dumplings:
   - Steaming Method: Arrange the filled dumplings in a single layer in a steamer basket lined with parchment paper or cabbage leaves. Steam over boiling water for 8-10 minutes until cooked through.
   - Pan-Frying Method: Heat a non-stick skillet over medium heat. Add a small amount of oil to coat the bottom of the skillet. Place the dumplings in the skillet, flat side down. Cook for 2-3 minutes until the bottoms are golden brown. Then, carefully add water to the skillet (about 1/4 cup) and cover immediately to steam the dumplings until the water evaporates.
4. Make the Dipping Sauce (Optional):
   - In a small bowl, mix together soy sauce, rice vinegar, and sesame oil.
   - Add chopped green onions or a drizzle of chili oil for extra flavor and heat.
5. Serve and Enjoy:
   - Once cooked, serve the tofu chive dumplings hot with the dipping sauce on the side.
   - Enjoy these delicious dumplings as a snack, appetizer, or part of a meal.

These tofu chive dumplings are versatile and can be customized with your favorite fillings and seasonings. Experiment with different dipping sauces and cooking methods to suit your taste preferences. They're perfect for sharing with family and friends!

Tofu and Sweet Potato Hash

Ingredients:

- 14 oz (400g) firm tofu, drained and pressed
- 2 medium sweet potatoes, peeled and diced
- 1 onion, diced
- 1 bell pepper (any color), diced
- 2 tablespoons olive oil
- 2 cloves garlic, minced
- 1 teaspoon smoked paprika
- 1/2 teaspoon ground cumin
- Salt and pepper, to taste
- Fresh parsley or green onions, chopped (for garnish)

Instructions:

1. Prepare the Tofu:
    - Cut the pressed tofu into small cubes.
2. Cook the Sweet Potatoes:
    - Heat 1 tablespoon of olive oil in a large skillet or cast-iron pan over medium heat.
    - Add the diced sweet potatoes to the skillet and cook for about 8-10 minutes, stirring occasionally, until they are tender and slightly browned. Remove from the skillet and set aside.
3. Cook the Tofu:
    - In the same skillet, add the remaining tablespoon of olive oil.
    - Add the diced tofu to the skillet and cook for 5-7 minutes, stirring occasionally, until the tofu is golden and crispy on all sides.
4. Combine the Ingredients:
    - Push the tofu to one side of the skillet and add the diced onion and bell pepper to the empty space.
    - Cook for 3-4 minutes until the vegetables are softened.
5. Season the Hash:
    - Stir in the minced garlic, smoked paprika, and ground cumin. Cook for 1 minute until fragrant.
    - Return the cooked sweet potatoes to the skillet and mix everything together.
    - Season with salt and pepper to taste.
6. Finish and Serve:

- Cook for another 2-3 minutes to allow the flavors to meld together.
- Remove from heat and garnish with chopped fresh parsley or green onions.
7. Serve the Tofu and Sweet Potato Hash:
    - Divide the hash onto plates or bowls.
    - Enjoy this delicious tofu and sweet potato hash as a hearty breakfast or brunch dish. You can also serve it with a side of scrambled eggs or a fresh salad.

This tofu and sweet potato hash is packed with flavor and textures, making it a satisfying and nutritious meal. Feel free to customize the hash with additional vegetables or spices based on your preferences. It's a versatile dish that's perfect for any time of day!

Tofu Miso Soup

Ingredients:

- 4 cups dashi stock (Japanese soup stock) or vegetable broth
- 8 oz (225g) firm tofu, cut into small cubes
- 2 tablespoons miso paste (white or red miso)
- 2 green onions, thinly sliced
- 1 sheet of nori (seaweed), cut into small pieces (optional)
- 1 tablespoon soy sauce (optional, for added flavor)
- 1 tablespoon mirin (optional, for a touch of sweetness)
- 1 tablespoon sesame oil (optional, for extra richness)
- 1 tablespoon wakame seaweed (dried) - rehydrated in water and drained (optional)
- Fresh cilantro or parsley, chopped (for garnish, optional)

Instructions:

1. Prepare the Dashi Stock:
    - If using dashi stock granules or powder, dissolve them in hot water according to package instructions. Alternatively, you can use vegetable broth as a substitute for dashi stock.
2. Add Tofu and Wakame (Seaweed):
    - Once the stock is ready and simmering, add the cubed tofu and rehydrated wakame seaweed (if using). Allow it to cook for 2-3 minutes until the tofu is heated through.
3. Dissolve Miso Paste:
    - In a small bowl, dissolve miso paste in a ladleful of the hot stock from the pot. Use a spoon to mix and dissolve the miso paste completely until smooth.
4. Add Miso Paste to Soup:
    - Lower the heat to low and gently stir in the dissolved miso paste into the soup. Avoid boiling the soup once miso paste has been added to preserve its flavor.
    - Add soy sauce, mirin, and sesame oil (if using) for additional flavor. Adjust seasoning to taste.
5. Add Green Onions and Nori:
    - Add sliced green onions and pieces of nori (seaweed) to the soup. Stir gently to combine.
6. Serve the Tofu Miso Soup:

- Ladle the hot tofu miso soup into individual serving bowls.
- Garnish with chopped fresh cilantro or parsley (if using).
7. Enjoy Your Tofu Miso Soup:
    - Serve the tofu miso soup hot and enjoy it as a comforting and nourishing dish.

Tofu miso soup is best enjoyed fresh and hot. It's a versatile dish, so feel free to adjust the ingredients and seasoning based on your preferences. You can also add other ingredients like mushrooms, spinach, or sliced carrots to customize the soup. Serve the tofu miso soup as a light and satisfying meal on its own or as part of a larger Japanese-inspired meal. Enjoy!

Tofu Pesto Pasta

Ingredients:

- 8 oz (225g) pasta of your choice (such as spaghetti, fettuccine, or penne)
- 14 oz (400g) firm tofu, drained and pressed
- 1/2 cup basil pesto (homemade or store-bought)
- 2 tablespoons olive oil
- 2 cloves garlic, minced
- Salt and pepper, to taste
- Grated Parmesan cheese or nutritional yeast, for serving (optional)
- Fresh basil leaves, chopped, for garnish (optional)

Instructions:

1. Cook the Pasta:
    - Bring a large pot of salted water to a boil. Cook the pasta according to the package instructions until al dente. Drain and set aside, reserving some pasta water.
2. Prepare the Tofu:
    - While the pasta is cooking, cut the pressed tofu into small cubes or strips.
3. Cook the Tofu:
    - Heat olive oil in a large skillet over medium-high heat.
    - Add minced garlic to the skillet and sauté for 1 minute until fragrant.
    - Add the tofu cubes to the skillet and cook for 5-7 minutes, stirring occasionally, until golden and crispy on all sides.
    - Season the tofu with salt and pepper to taste.
4. Combine Tofu and Pesto:
    - Lower the heat to medium and add the cooked pasta to the skillet with the tofu.
    - Add basil pesto to the skillet and toss everything together until the pasta and tofu are coated evenly with the pesto sauce.
    - If the pasta seems dry, add a splash of reserved pasta water to loosen the sauce.
5. Serve the Tofu Pesto Pasta:
    - Divide the tofu pesto pasta into serving bowls.
    - Optionally, sprinkle grated Parmesan cheese or nutritional yeast on top.
    - Garnish with chopped fresh basil leaves for extra flavor and freshness.
6. Enjoy Your Tofu Pesto Pasta:
    - Serve the tofu pesto pasta hot and enjoy this creamy and flavorful dish!

This tofu pesto pasta is quick and easy to make, perfect for a weeknight dinner or lunch. The crispy tofu adds a delightful texture to the creamy basil pesto sauce. Feel free to customize the dish by adding cherry tomatoes, spinach, or pine nuts for extra flavor and nutrition. Enjoy!

Tofu Stuffed Peppers

Ingredients:

- 4 large bell peppers (any color), tops cut off and seeds removed
- 14 oz (400g) firm tofu, drained and pressed
- 1 cup cooked quinoa or rice
- 1 onion, finely chopped
- 2 cloves garlic, minced
- 1 cup chopped spinach or kale
- 1 teaspoon dried oregano
- 1 teaspoon dried basil
- 1/2 teaspoon paprika
- Salt and pepper, to taste
- 1/2 cup grated cheese (such as mozzarella or cheddar), optional
- 2 tablespoons olive oil

Instructions:

1. Preheat the Oven:
   - Preheat your oven to 375°F (190°C).
2. Prepare the Bell Peppers:
   - Cut the tops off the bell peppers and remove the seeds and membranes from inside. Place the hollowed-out peppers in a baking dish.
3. Prepare the Filling:
   - In a large skillet, heat olive oil over medium heat.
   - Add chopped onion and minced garlic to the skillet. Sauté for 2-3 minutes until the onion is translucent.
4. Add Tofu to the Skillet:
   - Crumble the pressed tofu into the skillet using your hands or a fork. Cook for 5-6 minutes, stirring occasionally, until the tofu starts to brown and crisp up slightly.
5. Add Spinach (or Kale) and Seasonings:
   - Add chopped spinach or kale to the skillet. Cook for another 2-3 minutes until wilted.
   - Stir in cooked quinoa or rice, dried oregano, dried basil, paprika, salt, and pepper. Mix well to combine all ingredients.
   - If using grated cheese, mix half of it into the filling mixture and reserve the other half for topping.
6. Stuff the Peppers:

- Spoon the tofu and quinoa filling into the hollowed-out bell peppers, pressing down gently to fill them evenly.
7. Bake the Stuffed Peppers:
    - Sprinkle the remaining grated cheese on top of each stuffed pepper, if desired.
    - Cover the baking dish with foil and place it in the preheated oven.
    - Bake for 25-30 minutes, then remove the foil and bake for an additional 10 minutes until the peppers are tender and the filling is heated through.
8. Serve the Tofu Stuffed Peppers:
    - Remove the stuffed peppers from the oven and let them cool slightly before serving.
    - Garnish with fresh herbs like chopped parsley or basil, if desired.
    - Serve the tofu stuffed peppers hot as a wholesome and flavorful vegetarian meal.

Feel free to adjust the seasonings and ingredients according to your taste preferences.

These tofu stuffed peppers are nutritious, filling, and perfect for a family dinner or special occasion. Enjoy!

Tofu Caesar Wraps

Ingredients:

- 14 oz (400g) firm tofu, drained and pressed
- 4 large tortilla wraps (whole wheat or your choice)
- 1 head of romaine lettuce, washed and chopped
- 1/2 cup grated Parmesan cheese (use vegan Parmesan if preferred)
- Caesar dressing (store-bought or homemade)
- Salt and pepper, to taste
- Olive oil, for cooking

Instructions:

1. Prepare the Tofu:
    - Slice the pressed tofu into thin strips or cubes.
    - Season the tofu with salt and pepper.
2. Cook the Tofu:
    - Heat a skillet over medium-high heat and add a drizzle of olive oil.
    - Add the seasoned tofu to the skillet and cook for 3-4 minutes on each side, or until golden brown and crispy. Remove from heat and set aside.
3. Assemble the Wraps:
    - Lay out a tortilla wrap on a clean surface.
    - Spread a generous amount of Caesar dressing over the tortilla.
    - Arrange a handful of chopped romaine lettuce on top of the dressing.
    - Place a portion of the cooked tofu on the lettuce.
    - Sprinkle grated Parmesan cheese over the tofu.
4. Wrap the Tortilla:
    - Fold in the sides of the tortilla, then roll it up tightly from the bottom to form a wrap.
5. Serve the Tofu Caesar Wraps:
    - Repeat the process with the remaining tortillas and ingredients.
    - Optionally, slice the wraps in half diagonally before serving.
    - Serve the tofu Caesar wraps immediately and enjoy!

Homemade Caesar Dressing Recipe:

If you prefer to make your own Caesar dressing, here's a simple recipe:

Ingredients:

- 1/2 cup mayonnaise (regular or vegan)
- 2 tablespoons freshly squeezed lemon juice
- 2 teaspoons Dijon mustard
- 2 cloves garlic, minced
- 1/4 cup grated Parmesan cheese (use vegan Parmesan if preferred)
- Salt and pepper, to taste

Instructions:

1. In a bowl, whisk together mayonnaise, lemon juice, Dijon mustard, minced garlic, and grated Parmesan cheese until smooth and well combined.
2. Season with salt and pepper to taste.
3. Use as a dressing for the tofu Caesar wraps or store in the refrigerator for future use.

Feel free to customize these tofu Caesar wraps by adding additional toppings such as cherry tomatoes, croutons, or avocado slices. They make a delicious and convenient meal for lunch or a light dinner. Enjoy!

Tofu Kimchi Fried Rice

Ingredients:

- 14 oz (400g) firm tofu, drained and pressed
- 2 cups cooked rice (preferably day-old rice)
- 1 cup kimchi, chopped
- 1 onion, finely chopped
- 2-3 cloves garlic, minced
- 1 tablespoon soy sauce
- 1 tablespoon gochujang (Korean chili paste), optional for spice
- 1 tablespoon sesame oil
- 2 green onions, sliced (for garnish)
- Salt and pepper, to taste
- 1 tablespoon vegetable oil, for cooking

Instructions:

1. Prepare the Tofu:
    - Cut the pressed tofu into small cubes.
2. Cook the Tofu:
    - Heat vegetable oil in a large skillet or wok over medium-high heat.
    - Add the tofu cubes to the skillet and cook for 5-7 minutes, stirring occasionally, until golden and crispy on all sides.
    - Remove the tofu from the skillet and set aside.
3. Stir-Fry the Vegetables:
    - In the same skillet, add a bit more oil if needed.
    - Add chopped onion and minced garlic to the skillet. Sauté for 2-3 minutes until the onion is translucent.
4. Add Kimchi and Rice:
    - Add chopped kimchi to the skillet. Stir-fry for another 2 minutes.
    - Add cooked rice to the skillet, breaking up any clumps with a spatula.
5. Season the Fried Rice:
    - Drizzle soy sauce, gochujang (if using), and sesame oil over the rice mixture. Stir well to combine.
    - Season with salt and pepper to taste.
6. Combine Tofu with Fried Rice:
    - Add the cooked tofu back to the skillet with the fried rice mixture.
    - Stir everything together and cook for another 2-3 minutes until heated through.

7. Serve Tofu Kimchi Fried Rice:
    - Remove the skillet from heat.
    - Garnish with sliced green onions.
8. Enjoy Your Tofu Kimchi Fried Rice:
    - Serve the tofu kimchi fried rice hot as a delicious and satisfying meal.

Feel free to adjust the amount of kimchi and seasoning according to your taste preferences. This tofu kimchi fried rice is a great way to enjoy the bold flavors of Korean cuisine in a quick and easy dish. Serve it on its own or with additional side dishes for a complete meal. Enjoy!

Tofu and Eggplant Parmesan

Ingredients:

- 1 large eggplant, sliced into 1/4-inch rounds
- 14 oz (400g) firm tofu, drained and pressed
- 1 cup breadcrumbs (regular or panko)
- 1/2 cup grated Parmesan cheese (use vegan Parmesan if preferred)
- 2 eggs, beaten (or use a plant-based egg substitute)
- Salt and pepper, to taste
- Olive oil, for frying
- 2 cups marinara sauce
- 1 cup shredded mozzarella cheese (or vegan cheese)
- Fresh basil leaves, chopped, for garnish (optional)

Instructions:

1. Prepare the Eggplant and Tofu:
    - Slice the eggplant into 1/4-inch rounds. Sprinkle the eggplant slices with salt and let them sit for 15-20 minutes to draw out excess moisture. Pat dry with paper towels.
    - Cut the pressed tofu into slices or cubes.
2. Coat the Eggplant and Tofu:
    - In one shallow bowl, place the beaten eggs (or plant-based egg substitute).
    - In another shallow bowl, combine the breadcrumbs, grated Parmesan cheese, salt, and pepper.
    - Dip each eggplant slice and tofu piece into the beaten eggs, then coat with the breadcrumb mixture, pressing gently to adhere.
3. Fry the Eggplant and Tofu:
    - Heat olive oil in a large skillet over medium heat.
    - Fry the eggplant slices and tofu pieces in batches until golden and crispy on both sides, about 3-4 minutes per side. Add more oil as needed. Transfer to a paper towel-lined plate to drain excess oil.
4. Assemble the Parmesan:
    - Preheat your oven to 375°F (190°C).
    - Spread a thin layer of marinara sauce in the bottom of a baking dish.
    - Arrange a layer of fried eggplant slices in the dish, followed by a layer of crispy tofu pieces.
    - Top with more marinara sauce and shredded mozzarella cheese.

5. Bake the Parmesan:
   - Cover the baking dish with foil and bake for 20-25 minutes, or until the cheese is melted and bubbly.
6. Serve the Tofu and Eggplant Parmesan:
   - Remove from the oven and let it rest for a few minutes.
   - Garnish with chopped fresh basil leaves, if desired.
   - Serve the tofu and eggplant parmesan hot as a delicious vegetarian main course.

This tofu and eggplant parmesan is perfect served with a side of pasta or crusty bread. It's a comforting and satisfying dish that's sure to be enjoyed by everyone at the table. Feel free to customize it with your favorite marinara sauce and cheese. Enjoy!

Tofu Meatballs

Ingredients:

- 14 oz (400g) firm tofu, drained and pressed
- 1/2 cup breadcrumbs (regular or panko)
- 1/4 cup grated Parmesan cheese (use vegan Parmesan if preferred)
- 2 cloves garlic, minced
- 1/4 cup finely chopped onion
- 2 tablespoons chopped fresh parsley (or 1 tablespoon dried parsley)
- 1 tablespoon soy sauce or tamari
- 1 tablespoon tomato paste
- 1 teaspoon dried oregano
- 1/2 teaspoon dried basil
- Salt and pepper, to taste
- Olive oil, for baking or frying

Instructions:

1. Preheat the Oven:
    - Preheat your oven to 375°F (190°C) if baking the tofu meatballs.
2. Prepare the Tofu:
    - In a large mixing bowl, crumble the pressed tofu using your hands or a fork.
3. Combine Ingredients:
    - Add breadcrumbs, grated Parmesan cheese, minced garlic, chopped onion, chopped parsley, soy sauce, tomato paste, dried oregano, dried basil, salt, and pepper to the crumbled tofu. Mix well to combine all ingredients.
4. Form the Meatballs:
    - Take small portions of the tofu mixture and roll them into balls using your hands. The mixture should hold together well due to the breadcrumbs and tofu consistency.
5. Cook the Tofu Meatballs:
    - Baking Method: Place the tofu meatballs on a lightly greased baking sheet. Drizzle or brush the tops with olive oil. Bake in the preheated oven for 25-30 minutes, turning halfway through, until golden brown and crispy.
    - Frying Method: Heat olive oil in a skillet over medium heat. Add the tofu meatballs in batches and cook for 3-4 minutes per side, until golden brown and crispy. Transfer to a plate lined with paper towels to drain excess oil.

6. Serve the Tofu Meatballs:
   - Serve the tofu meatballs hot as desired. They can be enjoyed with marinara sauce and pasta, in sandwiches, as appetizers with dipping sauce, or any way you prefer!

These tofu meatballs are flavorful and can be easily customized with your favorite herbs and spices. They are a delicious plant-based alternative to traditional meatballs and can be enjoyed by vegans and non-vegans alike. Experiment with different sauces and sides to create a delightful meal!

Tofu Cacciatore

Ingredients:

- 14 oz (400g) firm tofu, drained and pressed
- 2 tablespoons olive oil
- 1 onion, chopped
- 2 bell peppers (any color), sliced
- 3 cloves garlic, minced
- 1 can (14 oz/400g) diced tomatoes
- 1 can (6 oz/170g) tomato paste
- 1 teaspoon dried oregano
- 1 teaspoon dried basil
- 1/2 teaspoon dried thyme
- Salt and pepper, to taste
- Red pepper flakes (optional, for heat)
- Fresh basil or parsley, chopped, for garnish

Instructions:

1. Prepare the Tofu:
    - Cut the pressed tofu into cubes or strips.
2. Sauté the Tofu:
    - Heat 1 tablespoon of olive oil in a large skillet over medium-high heat.
    - Add the tofu cubes to the skillet and cook until golden and crispy on all sides, about 5-7 minutes. Remove the tofu from the skillet and set aside.
3. Cook the Vegetables:
    - In the same skillet, heat the remaining tablespoon of olive oil over medium heat.
    - Add chopped onion and sliced bell peppers to the skillet. Sauté for 5-7 minutes until the vegetables are softened.
4. Add Garlic and Tomatoes:
    - Add minced garlic to the skillet and cook for 1 minute until fragrant.
    - Stir in diced tomatoes, tomato paste, dried oregano, dried basil, dried thyme, salt, pepper, and red pepper flakes (if using). Mix well to combine.
5. Simmer the Sauce:
    - Bring the sauce to a simmer. Reduce heat to low and let it simmer for 15-20 minutes to allow the flavors to meld and the sauce to thicken slightly.
6. Add Tofu Back to the Skillet:

- Add the cooked tofu back to the skillet with the sauce. Stir gently to coat the tofu with the sauce.
7. Serve Tofu Cacciatore:
    - Remove the skillet from heat.
    - Garnish with chopped fresh basil or parsley.
    - Serve the tofu cacciatore hot over cooked pasta, rice, quinoa, or crusty bread.
8. Enjoy Your Tofu Cacciatore:
    - Serve this delicious vegan dish as a main course for a satisfying and flavorful meal.

Feel free to customize this tofu cacciatore by adding extra vegetables such as mushrooms, zucchini, or carrots. The savory tomato-based sauce pairs beautifully with the crispy tofu, creating a comforting and satisfying dish. Enjoy!

Tofu Sloppy Joes

Ingredients:

- 14 oz (400g) firm tofu, drained and pressed
- 1 tablespoon olive oil
- 1 onion, finely chopped
- 2 cloves garlic, minced
- 1 bell pepper, finely chopped (any color)
- 1 can (14 oz/400g) crushed tomatoes
- 2 tablespoons tomato paste
- 2 tablespoons soy sauce or tamari
- 1 tablespoon maple syrup or brown sugar
- 1 tablespoon apple cider vinegar
- 1 teaspoon chili powder
- 1/2 teaspoon smoked paprika
- Salt and pepper, to taste
- Hamburger buns or cooked rice, for serving

Instructions:

1. Prepare the Tofu:
   - Crumble the pressed tofu into small pieces resembling ground meat.
2. Sauté the Vegetables:
   - Heat olive oil in a large skillet over medium heat.
   - Add chopped onion and bell pepper to the skillet. Sauté for 5-7 minutes until softened.
3. Add Garlic and Tofu:
   - Add minced garlic to the skillet and cook for 1 minute until fragrant.
   - Add the crumbled tofu to the skillet. Cook for 5-7 minutes, stirring occasionally, until the tofu starts to brown and crisp up slightly.
4. Make the Sauce:
   - In a small bowl, whisk together crushed tomatoes, tomato paste, soy sauce or tamari, maple syrup or brown sugar, apple cider vinegar, chili powder, smoked paprika, salt, and pepper.
5. Simmer Everything Together:
   - Pour the sauce mixture over the tofu and vegetables in the skillet. Stir well to combine.

- Bring the mixture to a simmer. Reduce heat to low and let it simmer for 10-15 minutes, stirring occasionally, to allow the flavors to meld and the sauce to thicken.
6. Adjust Seasoning:
    - Taste and adjust seasoning as needed, adding more salt, pepper, or chili powder according to your preference.
7. Serve Tofu Sloppy Joes:
    - Toast hamburger buns if desired.
    - Spoon the tofu sloppy joe mixture onto the buns.
    - Alternatively, serve the tofu sloppy joes over cooked rice or your favorite grain.
8. Enjoy Your Tofu Sloppy Joes:
    - Serve these delicious and flavorful tofu sloppy joes hot, garnished with pickles, sliced onions, or coleslaw if desired.

This tofu sloppy joe recipe is a fantastic plant-based alternative that's packed with protein and flavor. It's a perfect family-friendly meal that can be enjoyed any day of the week!

Tofu Spinach Lasagna

Ingredients:

- 12 lasagna noodles, cooked according to package instructions
- 14 oz (400g) firm tofu, drained and pressed
- 1 package (10 oz/280g) frozen chopped spinach, thawed and squeezed dry
- 2 cups marinara sauce
- 1 cup shredded mozzarella cheese (use vegan cheese if preferred)
- 1/2 cup grated Parmesan cheese (use vegan Parmesan if preferred)
- 2 cloves garlic, minced
- 1 tablespoon olive oil
- 1 teaspoon dried oregano
- Salt and pepper, to taste
- Fresh basil leaves, chopped, for garnish (optional)

Instructions:

1. Preheat the Oven:
    - Preheat your oven to 375°F (190°C).
2. Prepare the Tofu Filling:
    - In a large bowl, crumble the pressed tofu using your hands or a fork.
    - Add minced garlic, dried oregano, salt, and pepper to the crumbled tofu.
    - Mix well to combine.
    - Add the thawed and squeezed dry spinach to the tofu mixture. Mix until evenly combined.
3. Assemble the Lasagna:
    - Spread a thin layer of marinara sauce on the bottom of a 9x13-inch baking dish.
    - Arrange a layer of cooked lasagna noodles on top of the sauce.
    - Spread half of the tofu and spinach mixture over the noodles.
    - Sprinkle half of the shredded mozzarella cheese and grated Parmesan cheese over the tofu mixture.
    - Repeat with another layer of marinara sauce, noodles, remaining tofu and spinach mixture, and remaining shredded mozzarella and Parmesan cheeses.
    - Finish with a final layer of marinara sauce and a sprinkle of grated Parmesan cheese on top.
4. Bake the Lasagna:

- Cover the baking dish with foil and bake in the preheated oven for 30 minutes.
- Remove the foil and bake for an additional 10-15 minutes, or until the lasagna is bubbly and the cheese is melted and golden brown on top.

5. Let Rest and Serve:
   - Remove the lasagna from the oven and let it rest for 10 minutes before slicing.
   - Garnish with chopped fresh basil leaves, if desired.
   - Serve the tofu spinach lasagna hot, and enjoy!

This tofu spinach lasagna is a comforting and satisfying dish that's perfect for family dinners or gatherings. It's packed with flavor, protein, and nutrients from the tofu and spinach. Feel free to customize it with additional vegetables or herbs to suit your taste. Serve with a side salad or garlic bread for a complete meal. Enjoy!

Tofu Pita Pockets

Ingredients:

- 14 oz (400g) firm tofu, drained and pressed
- 4 whole wheat pita bread rounds
- 1 cup shredded lettuce or mixed greens
- 1 tomato, sliced
- 1 cucumber, sliced
- 1/2 red onion, thinly sliced
- Hummus, store-bought or homemade
- Tzatziki sauce, store-bought or homemade (optional)
- Olive oil
- Salt and pepper, to taste
- Lemon juice (optional)

Instructions:

1. Prepare the Tofu:
    - Slice the pressed tofu into thin strips or cubes.
2. Cook the Tofu:
    - Heat a drizzle of olive oil in a skillet over medium-high heat.
    - Add the tofu slices or cubes to the skillet.
    - Season with salt and pepper.
    - Cook for 5-7 minutes, stirring occasionally, until the tofu is golden and crispy on all sides.
    - Optional: Squeeze a little lemon juice over the tofu for added flavor.
3. Assemble the Pita Pockets:
    - Warm the pita bread rounds in a toaster oven or microwave for a few seconds to make them pliable.
    - Spread a generous amount of hummus inside each pita pocket.
    - Fill each pita pocket with shredded lettuce or mixed greens, sliced tomato, cucumber, red onion, and cooked tofu.
4. Add Tzatziki Sauce (Optional):
    - If using tzatziki sauce, drizzle some over the filling inside the pita pockets.
5. Serve and Enjoy:
    - Serve the tofu pita pockets immediately.
    - Enjoy these flavorful and nutritious pockets as a quick and satisfying meal.

Feel free to customize your tofu pita pockets with other vegetables or sauces of your choice, such as roasted bell peppers, olives, or hot sauce. They make a great lunch or dinner option for when you're on the go or looking for a light and tasty meal. Enjoy!

Tofu Waldorf Salad

Ingredients:

- 14 oz (400g) firm tofu, drained and pressed
- 2 celery stalks, diced
- 1 apple, diced (choose a sweet variety like Fuji or Gala)
- 1/2 cup red seedless grapes, halved
- 1/4 cup chopped walnuts or pecans
- 1/4 cup dried cranberries or raisins
- 1/4 cup vegan mayonnaise (or regular mayonnaise if not vegan)
- 1 tablespoon Dijon mustard
- 1 tablespoon lemon juice
- 1 tablespoon maple syrup or honey (optional)
- Salt and pepper, to taste
- Fresh parsley or cilantro, chopped (for garnish)

Instructions:

1. Prepare the Tofu:
   - Cut the pressed tofu into small cubes.
2. Cook the Tofu (Optional):
   - You can either use the tofu as is (raw) or lightly pan-fry the tofu cubes for a few minutes in a skillet with a bit of oil until golden and crispy. Let cool slightly.
3. Prepare the Salad Dressing:
   - In a small bowl, whisk together the vegan mayonnaise (or regular mayonnaise), Dijon mustard, lemon juice, maple syrup or honey (if using), salt, and pepper. Adjust the seasoning to taste.
4. Assemble the Salad:
   - In a large mixing bowl, combine the diced celery, diced apple, halved grapes, chopped nuts, and dried cranberries or raisins.
   - Add the cooked or raw tofu cubes to the bowl.
5. Add the Dressing:
   - Pour the salad dressing over the tofu and vegetable mixture.
   - Gently toss everything together until well combined and evenly coated with the dressing.
6. Chill and Serve:

- Cover the bowl with plastic wrap or a lid and refrigerate the tofu Waldorf salad for at least 30 minutes to allow the flavors to meld and the salad to chill.
7. Garnish and Enjoy:
    - Before serving, garnish the tofu Waldorf salad with chopped fresh parsley or cilantro.
    - Serve the salad chilled as a delicious and satisfying meal or side dish.

This tofu Waldorf salad is perfect for lunch, picnics, or potlucks. It's packed with flavor and textures from the crunchy celery, sweet apples, juicy grapes, and creamy tofu. Feel free to customize the salad by adding other ingredients such as chopped lettuce, sliced almonds, or a sprinkle of cinnamon. Enjoy!

Tofu Lemon Bars

Ingredients:

For the Crust:

- 1 1/2 cups graham cracker crumbs (or crushed cookies of choice)
- 1/4 cup granulated sugar
- 6 tablespoons melted butter or vegan butter

For the Filling:

- 14 oz (400g) firm tofu, drained and pressed
- 3/4 cup granulated sugar
- Zest of 2 lemons
- 1/2 cup freshly squeezed lemon juice (about 3-4 lemons)
- 2 tablespoons cornstarch
- 1/4 teaspoon turmeric (optional, for color)
- Powdered sugar, for dusting (optional)

Instructions:

1. Preheat the Oven:
    - Preheat your oven to 350°F (175°C). Grease an 8x8-inch baking dish or line it with parchment paper.
2. Make the Crust:
    - In a mixing bowl, combine the graham cracker crumbs, sugar, and melted butter.
    - Press the mixture evenly into the bottom of the prepared baking dish.
    - Bake the crust for 10 minutes, then remove it from the oven and set aside to cool.
3. Prepare the Filling:
    - In a food processor or blender, combine the drained and pressed tofu, granulated sugar, lemon zest, lemon juice, cornstarch, and turmeric (if using).
    - Blend until smooth and creamy, scraping down the sides as needed to ensure everything is well combined.
4. Assemble and Bake:
    - Pour the tofu lemon filling over the cooled crust in the baking dish.

- Spread the filling into an even layer with a spatula.
- Bake for 25-30 minutes, or until the edges are set and the filling is slightly firm to the touch.

5. Chill and Serve:
   - Remove the baking dish from the oven and let it cool completely at room temperature.
   - Once cooled, transfer the dish to the refrigerator and chill for at least 2 hours, or until the filling is fully set.
6. Slice and Garnish:
   - When ready to serve, use a sharp knife to slice the chilled tofu lemon bars into squares.
   - Dust with powdered sugar if desired before serving.
7. Enjoy Your Tofu Lemon Bars:
   - Serve the tofu lemon bars chilled as a refreshing and tangy dessert.

These tofu lemon bars are creamy, zesty, and perfect for lemon lovers. The tofu adds a silky texture to the filling while keeping the bars light and refreshing. They make a wonderful treat for special occasions or as a sweet ending to any meal. Enjoy!

www.ingramcontent.com/pod-product-compliance
Lightning Source LLC
LaVergne TN
LVHW081601060526
838201LV00054B/2017